WHAT IS TO BE DONE?

NAPOLEON CHANDRAGUPTA
MANJUNATH

Published by True Sign Publishing House
Address: 21, 2nd Floor, Kundan Nagar, Bagmugaliya,
Bhopal, Madhya Pradesh - 462026
E-mail: truesignbooks@gmail.com
Website: www.truesign.in

What Is To Be Done?

Author: Napoleon Chandragupta Manjunath

ISBN: 978-93-6253-092-9

First Edition: 2024

"There are decades where nothing happens;

and there are weeks where decades happen."

-Vladimir Lenin

Napoleon Chandragupta Manjunath

Indian revolutionary, existential philosopher, absurdist, anti-corruption activist, working towards the unification of India, and advocating for the integration of the global community.

CONTENTS

Preface

Harmonies of Transformation

In the grand symphony of human existence, this book, "What Is To Be Done," serves as a melodic exploration into the pulsating rhythms of struggle, aspiration, and the ceaseless pursuit of a brighter horizon. As we embark on this intellectual odyssey, we venture into the heart of societal dilemmas, the corridors of political ideologies, and the rustic landscapes where individuals shape their destinies.

The narrative unfolds with the resonant cadence of societal challenges and aspirations. Listen closely, and you'll hear the echoes of our collective struggles, the clatter of our aspirations, and the rhythm of resilience that beats beneath the surface of our daily lives.

In the political amphitheatre, we pose the question, "What is the path forward?" Here, the intellectual crescendo builds as we unravel the visions of those who contemplate the road to a society where equity and justice are not just ideals but concrete realities. The pages unfurl to reveal the goals, ideologies, and pathways envisioned by these architects of societal change.

Journeying through diverse landscapes, we traverse territories marked by the stark dichotomy of privilege and deprivation, the powerful and the marginalized. At the crossroads of morality, individuals contemplate their allegiance to entrenched systems or their solidarity with the marginalized masses.

The narrative unfolds further, revealing the comprehensive improvements sought by visionaries for the greater good. From the sweeping vistas of societal change to the nuanced struggles within different sectors, each chapter contributes to the symphony of transformation

As the narrative crescendos, we scrutinize the complexities of contemporary challenges, dissect the demerits of existing systems, and explore the multifaceted journey towards change. The responsibilities of citizens and the cultural refrains surrounding pivotal issues emerge as profound movements within our symphony of transformation.

"What Is To Be Done" extends an invitation not just to read but to partake in the harmonies of transformation. It beckons readers to engage critically with societal structures, contemplating the harmonies that can lead us towards a more just and equitable future.

In the spirit of inquiry and dialogue, let us embark together on this intellectual symphony, harmonizing diverse perspectives and collectively seeking the transformative chords that bind us in our shared humanity.

1

Centralization of Means of Communication, Education, Health-care, Jobs and Transport

1. Communication:

- **Centralized Communication Infrastructure:** Establishing a centralized communication infrastructure could involve nationalizing or centralizing major communication channels, ensuring equitable access and possibly controlling content dissemination.

- **Media and Information Control:** There is implications for media independence, freedom of the press and control of information. Striking a balance between centralized control and freedom of expression would be crucial.

2. Education:

- **Centralized Curriculum and Standards:** A centralized education system might entail a uniform national curriculum and standardized education standards. This could ensure consistency but might limit local variations and innovation.

- **Resource Allocation:** Centralized control involve a more uniform allocation of resources across regions, aiming to address educational disparities.

3. Health-care:

- **Nationalized Health--care System:** Centralizing health-care could involve a nationalized health-care system, ensuring equal access to medical services. It will address regional health disparities.

4. Jobs:

- **Centralized Job Planning:** Centralized job planning involves the government playing a significant role in job creation, allocation and career planning.

5. Transport:

- National Transport Network: Centralizing transport infrastructure might involve the creation and management of a national transportation network. This could enhance connectivity but would require substantial investment and coordination.

  The importance of centralizing the means of communication and transport under the control of the poor. This centralization is seen as a way to eliminate the fragmented nature of capitalist production.

6. Equal Liability of All to Work:

In a socialist society, a system where all individuals contribute to societal production according to their abilities. The principle "from each according to his ability, to each according to his needs" reflects this idea.

7. Abolition of Family Inheritance:

The abolition of the traditional rich family structure. It is believed that the family, as an institution, was shaped by the capitalist mode of production and would be transformed in a Socialist society.

8. International Character of the Revolution:

The international character of the revolution. We believed that workers of all countries must unite to overthrow the capitalists, rich and establish global unity by means of Manjunathism.

2

Demerits of Caste System in India and why we should eliminate Caste System in India?

If the institution of caste has been of great value to Hinduism, it has also been responsible for a good many evils. According to, "The caste system has acted essentially to impose that attitude of mind, needed to raise men from savagery but to stop them half way on progress." Some of the demerits of the caste system are as follows:

1. A Disintegrating Factor:

A prominent disintegrating factor within Hindu society is the pervasive caste system, which has intricately partitioned the community into numerous hereditary castes and sub-castes. This system has inadvertently fostered a sense of exclusivity and class-based pride, leading to the compartmentalization of individuals and creating substantial divisions among different segments of the population.

The caste system's rigid structure has had the consequential effect of constraining people's perspectives, limiting their interactions and perpetuating social inequalities. Rather than fostering a sense of unity and collective identity, it has instead given rise to pronounced disparities, hindering the development of a shared national consciousness.

The stratification inherent in the caste system has led to the formation of distinct social strata, each with its own customs, traditions and privileges. This has, unfortunately, resulted in the widening of gulfs between various sections of the society, impeding the growth of a cohesive and inclusive national ethos.

In essence, rather than serving as an integrating force, the caste system has acted as a disintegrating influence within Hindu society. Its perpetuation has thwarted efforts to forge a unified identity, emphasizing individual caste affiliations over a broader sense of collective belonging. Addressing the challenges posed by the caste system becomes crucial for the fostering of a more integrated and harmonious society.

2. Check on Economic and Intellectual Advancement and Social Reforms:

The caste system, unfortunately, acts as a significant impediment to both economic and intellectual progress and serves as a formidable obstacle to social reforms. This is primarily because it confines economic and intellectual opportunities to specific sections of the population while denying them to others. This rigid structure hinders the free pursuit of education and professional endeavours, perpetuating inequalities and stifling individual potential.

Consider, for instance, the plight of individuals in occupations such as sweeping or cobbling. Despite possessing natural aptitude and the requisite physical and intellectual capabilities, these individuals are barred from pursuing educational or scientific professions due to the strictures of the caste system. This denial of opportunities based on one's birth rather than meritocracy is a grave injustice, preventing worthy and capable individuals from attaining their rightful places in society.

The inflexibility inherent in the caste system severely hampers the development of genius and curtails individual liberty. Initiative and enterprise are stifled, resulting in the suppression of human energy and talent. This untapped potential represents a significant loss to the community, hindering its cultural and civilizational progress.

In stark contrast to the democratic principles of modern societies that aim to provide equal opportunities for all, the caste system perpetuates a hierarchical structure that disregards talents based on birth rather than merit. This not only obstructs the growth of low-born talents but also shields high-born incompetents from the consequences of their shortcomings.

To foster a truly progressive and inclusive society, it is imperative to dismantle the rigid barriers imposed by the caste system. Embracing a system that values merit, encourages individual initiative and provides equal opportunities for all members of society will unlock untold potential, contributing to the enrichment of culture and civilization.

3. Denies Mobility of Labour:

In the realm of economics, the caste system poses a significant impediment to the optimal utilization of labour, hindering the seamless mobility of labour, capital and productive endeavours. This systemic barrier not only undermines the efficiency of the workforce but also stifles the potential for perfect mobility within economic sectors. The repercussions of such restrictions are multifaceted, manifesting in the stunted growth of large-scale industries and a suboptimal exploitation of the country's economic resources, all to the detriment of the nation's populace.

The caste system's rigidity, which stratifies individuals based on hereditary occupations, inhibits the free flow of labour to areas of highest demand and productivity. This lack of fluidity impedes the economy's ability to dynamically allocate human resources where they are most needed, thus limiting the efficiency and responsiveness of the labour market.

Moreover, the caste system encumbers the free movement of capital and productive efforts. The entrenched social divisions restrict individuals from venturing into occupations outside their hereditary caste-based occupations, hindering the diversification of skills and limiting the potential for innovation and entrepreneurship. This, in turn, constrains the development of a robust and diverse economic landscape.

The sub-optimal utilization of economic resources is a direct consequence of the caste system's influence on occupational choices and opportunities. The predetermined social roles restrict individuals from pursuing professions that align with their aptitudes and aspirations, resulting in a workforce that may not be aligned with the demands of emerging industries or evolving economic needs.

In conclusion, the caste system's pervasive influence not only hampers the efficiency of labour but also impedes the fluidity of capital and productive efforts. This, in turn, hinders the development of large-scale industries and prevents the nation from fully exploiting its economic resources for the collective benefit of its people. Addressing these systemic challenges is crucial for fostering a more dynamic and inclusive economic environment that can propel the nation towards greater prosperity and sustainable growth.

4. Exploits Lower Castes:

The caste system, deeply ingrained in the social fabric of Hindu society, perpetuates a cycle of exploitation that disproportionately affects the economically weaker and socially inferior castes. This entrenched social hierarchy serves to safeguard the privileges of the higher castes, contributing to the exacerbation of economic discontent and the reinforcement of social prejudices.

The system's inherent design creates a stark divide between the privileged and marginalized groups, limiting the upward mobility of those in economically disadvantaged castes. This not only results in the perpetuation of socio-economic inequality but also hampers the overall progress and inclusivity of the society.

Moreover, the proliferation of numerous castes, each bound by a rigid social code, has led to a considerable waste of resources, both in terms of time and energy. The imposition of various taboos, such as restrictions on cooking, eating and drinking, has created a complex web of prohibitions that, while deeply rooted in tradition, has become a source of inefficiency and impediment to individual freedom.

The inflexibility of the caste system further obstructs the adoption of progressive and modern ways of life. This resistance to change inhibits societal evolution and restrains the ability of individuals to adapt to newer paradigms, hindering the overall societal development.

Additionally, the caste system acts as a barrier to free association between Hindus and non-Hindus, limiting cross-cultural interactions and exchange of ideas. This isolation from diverse perspectives constrains the ability of the Hindu community to keep pace with the rapidly evolving global landscape, both socially and economically.

Addressing these challenges necessitates a revaluation of the caste system and a concerted effort towards fostering inclusivity, dismantling barriers and promoting equal opportunities. A more flexible and egalitarian social structure would not only contribute to economic and social progress but also enable Hindus to engage more meaningfully with the broader world, fostering a spirit of unity and shared growth.

5. Imposes Hardship on Women:

The caste system, deeply rooted in societal norms, has imposed immense hardships on women, subjecting them to a myriad of oppressive practices that have profoundly impacted their lives. Among these, the insistence on archaic customs such as child marriage, prohibition of widow remarriage and the seclusion of women has cast a shadow over the well-being and prospects of women, contributing to their prolonged suffering and deprivation.

Child marriage, a prevalent practice stemming from traditional norms, has subjected countless young girls to premature unions, denying them the opportunity for education and personal development. This early imposition of marital responsibilities often leads to adverse physical and mental health outcomes for young brides, perpetuating cycles of poverty and limiting their ability to lead empowered lives.

The prohibition of widow remarriage is another deeply entrenched practice that exacerbates the plight of women. Widows, often ostracized and marginalized, are denied the chance to rebuild their lives through marriage. This denial not only perpetuates their social isolation but also reinforces a sense of dependency, leaving them vulnerable to economic and social hardships.

The seclusion of women, often enforced through societal norms and expectations, restricts their freedom and participation in public life. This confinement limits opportunities for education, employment and social engagement, trapping women in a cycle of dependency and reinforcing traditional gender roles.

Moreover, the intersections of gender and caste discrimination compound the challenges faced by women in marginalized communities. Discrimination on the basis of both caste and gender further limits access to resources, opportunities and social support for women, exacerbating their vulnerability.

The cumulative impact of these practices has rendered the lives of women within the caste system profoundly miserable. It perpetuates a cycle of disempowerment, limiting their agency, stifling personal growth and hindering their contribution to broader societal development. Addressing these issues requires a comprehensive effort to challenge and dismantle the systemic barriers that perpetuate gender-based discrimination within the caste system, fostering an environment where women can lead lives characterized by dignity, equality and opportunity.

6. Perpetuates Untouchability:

The caste system has inflicted an enduring and deplorable legacy, consigning vast segments of society to lives marked by degradation and hopelessness, with the creation of untouchability standing out as a particularly egregious evil. As articulated by BR Ambedkar, untouchability embedded within Hindu society represents a unique and abhorrent phenomenon, unparalleled in its cruelty and exclusionary nature. This form of discrimination, absent in other human societies, stands as a dark stain on the tapestry of human culture.

The profound words of Ambedkar resonate with the stark reality that untouchability has cast upon millions, turning them into pariahs within their own communities. The heinous practice not only isolates individuals but also perpetuates a hierarchical system where certain groups are deemed so impure that mere proximity is considered contaminating. This deeply ingrained prejudice manifests in a myriad of ways, denying opportunities, basic human dignity and perpetuating social ostracization.

Mahatma Gandhi aptly characterizes untouchability as the "hate fullest expression of caste," emphasizing the corrosive impact of this practice on the very soul of the caste system. The discriminatory beliefs that underpin untouchability permeates every aspect of life, shaping social interactions, marriage prospects and economic opportunities, creating a pervasive atmosphere of exclusion.

Furthermore, large sections of society, deemed untouchable, find themselves relegated to a state akin to virtual slavery. Stripped of basic rights and opportunities, they are consigned to the margins of society, perpetuating cycles of poverty and disenfranchisement. This systemic injustice not only curtails individual freedoms but also stifles collective progress, as untouchables are denied the chance to contribute meaningfully to the societal fabric.

The eradication of untouchability demands a profound societal transformation, challenging ingrained prejudices and dismantling the structural barriers that sustain this form of discrimination. It necessitates an unwavering commitment to equality, justice and human dignity, fostering an inclusive society where every individual, regardless of caste, enjoys the full spectrum of rights and opportunities. Only through such transformative efforts can we hope to redeem the countless lives ensnared in the dehumanizing grip of untouchability and strive towards a more just and egalitarian future.

7. Creates the Feeling of Casteism:

The caste system has engendered a corrosive phenomenon known as casteism, a deeply ingrained sentiment wherein individuals harbour strong, exclusive loyalties to their own caste, often at the expense of broader social principles such as justice, fairness, equity and brotherhood. This manifestation of narrow group identity not only perpetuates division but also undermines the foundational values crucial for the establishment of a harmonious and egalitarian society.

Members of specific castes, influenced by the tenets of casteism, tend to prioritize their caste allegiance above considerations of broader societal welfare. This myopic perspective fosters an environment where individuals become blinded by loyalty to their caste, neglecting the principles of justice and fair play that should ideally guide interactions within a diverse society.

One of the profound impacts of casteism is the exploitation of these sentiments by politicians for their own gain, often at the detriment of the nation's interests. Politicians may strategically leverage caste affiliations to consolidate votes, creating a divisive political landscape that undermines the unity required for collective progress. This opportunistic manipulation of caste sentiments perpetuates a cycle of social fragmentation, hindering the development of a cohesive national identity.

As noted by **Ghurye,** the spirit of caste patriotism, a manifestation of casteism, fosters opposition between different castes and creates an atmosphere hostile to the growth of national consciousness. This divisive sentiment impedes the emergence of a unified national identity that transcends caste boundaries, hindering the development of collective goals and aspirations essential for the advancement of the nation as a whole.

To address these challenges, it becomes imperative to dismantle the divisive mind-set perpetuated by casteism. Encouraging a shift towards a more inclusive, egalitarian ethos requires not only legislative measures but also concerted efforts in education and awareness to promote a sense of shared identity and citizenship. By fostering an environment where individuals can transcend narrow caste loyalties and embrace a broader sense of unity, society can pave the way for the growth of a more robust national consciousness, fostering a collective commitment to justice, fairness and equity for all.

8. Results in Religious Conversion:

The caste system, with its inherent social hierarchies and entrenched inequalities, has unfortunately created conditions that sometimes lead to religious conversions, particularly among lower caste individuals. The pervasive discrimination and oppression faced by the lower castes have, at times, driven some to seek refuge in religions such as Islam and Christianity. This phenomenon is often a response to the perceived tyranny and injustice perpetuated by the upper castes.

The lower caste communities, historically subjected to social marginalization, economic exploitation and restricted access to basic resources, may view religious conversion as a pathway to escape the shackles of the caste system. Islam and Christianity, with their emphasis on equality and spiritual fraternity, can be perceived as alternatives that offer social dignity, equal status and a sense of belonging that may be lacking within the confines of the caste-based social order.

The process of conversion can be a complex interplay of socio-economic factors, as well as a response to the search for identity, dignity and social justice. It represents a way for individuals to assert their agency, breaking free from the oppressive structures that the caste system imposes.

Religious conversion, however, is not solely driven by the tyranny of the upper castes. It is a nuanced phenomenon influenced by a myriad of factors, including economic considerations, educational opportunities and social empowerment. While some individuals may see conversion as a means of escaping caste-based discrimination, others may choose it for personal spiritual reasons or a desire for a more inclusive and egalitarian community.

The complexity of the issue underscores the need for comprehensive social reforms that address the root causes of caste-based discrimination and provide avenues for social upliftment and empowerment. Initiatives promoting education, economic opportunities and social equality can contribute to dismantling the systemic injustices embedded in the caste

WHAT IS TO BE DONE ?

system, potentially mitigating the factors that drive individuals towards religious conversion. A holistic approach that fosters inclusivity, social justice and equal opportunities is essential for creating a society where individuals do not feel compelled to seek refuge in other religions due to the tyranny of caste-based oppression.

9. Stands in the way of Modernization:

The caste system serves as a formidable obstacle to the process of modernization, impeding the requisite transformation in outlook, mentality and socio-economic development essential for modernity. Modernization demands a departure from traditional norms and a shift towards a more progressive and inclusive societal framework. However, the caste system, with its rigid adherence to caste-based norms, poses a substantial hindrance to this transformative process.

The inherent nature of the caste system compels individuals to conform strictly to predetermined roles and norms, stifling the autonomy required for embracing modern ideas. This restriction on individual freedom impedes the evolution of a mind-set conducive to modernization, preventing the adoption of new perspectives, values and practices that characterize contemporary societies.

The limitations of the caste system have led to a sense of contrition among modern Indian intellectuals. The recognition of its shortcomings has fuelled a collective sentiment of hostility towards compromises that sustain the caste structure. As a result, there is a growing acknowledgment of the need for dismantling the barriers imposed by caste, fostering a more inclusive and progressive society.

Despite these criticisms, it is essential to acknowledge that the caste system, in its unique way, offers a place in society for various groups—be they racial, social, religious or occupational. It allows them to function as cooperating parts of the social whole without completely sacrificing their individual identity and distinctive character. This integrative aspect of the caste system, while being distinctive to India, raises questions about its effectiveness in promoting social cohesion and cooperation.

While the caste system may have certain integrative elements, its shortcomings in perpetuating social inequalities and impeding individual freedoms cannot be ignored. As India progresses in the contemporary era, there is a growing realization of the need for reforms that strike a balance between preserving cultural diversity and fostering a more egalitarian and forward-looking society. This ongoing discourse reflects the complex and multi-faceted nature of the caste system and its impact on India's modernization journey.

3

Why and how to eliminate Caste System?

Eliminating the caste system is a complex challenge that involves addressing deeply ingrained social, cultural and economic structures. Here are some reasons why and how the caste system should be eliminated:

1. Equality and Social Justice:

- **Reason:** The caste system is inherently discriminatory, perpetuating inequality and social injustice. It categorizes individuals into hierarchies, determining their social status, opportunities and privileges based on birth.

- **How:** Implementing policies and laws that promote equal rights, opportunities and access to resources for all individuals, regardless of their caste background, is crucial. Affirmative action programmes can help bridge historical gaps and create a more level playing field.

2. Economic Development:

- **Reason:** The caste system has implications for economic development, as it restricts access to opportunities and resources for certain castes. Breaking down these barriers is essential for fostering economic growth and reducing poverty.

- **How:** Implementing inclusive economic policies that focus on equitable distribution of resources, education and employment opportunities can help dismantle economic disparities associated with caste.

3. Social Harmony:

- **Reason:** The caste system fosters division and social disharmony, creating a fragmented society. Eliminating it is essential for building a cohesive and united nation.

- **How:** Encouraging inter-caste marriages, promoting cultural exchange, and fostering social integration initiatives can help break down caste-based barriers and promote unity.

4. Education and Awareness:

- **Reason:** Education is a powerful tool for challenging and dismantling deep-rooted beliefs associated with the caste system. Awareness campaigns can help change mind-sets and foster a more inclusive society.

- **How:** Implementing educational programmes that promote values of equality, tolerance and diversity can play a significant role. Creating awareness about the historical injustices and the impact of the caste system can lead to attitudinal changes.

5. Legal Reforms:

- **Reason:** Stringent legal measures are necessary to combat caste-based discrimination and violence. Strengthening anti-discrimination laws and ensuring their effective enforcement is crucial.

- **How:** Implementing and rigorously enforcing laws that criminalize caste-based discrimination, violence and hate crimes can act as a deterrent and provide legal recourse for victims.

6. Grassroots Initiatives:

- **Reason:** Change often starts at the grassroots level. Local community initiatives that promote inter-caste cooperation, dialogue and shared cultural experiences can contribute to dismantling the caste system.

- **How:** Supporting and empowering community-led initiatives that aim to break down caste barriers, promote dialogue and foster understanding can create positive change from the ground-up.

Eliminating the caste system requires a comprehensive and coordinated effort that addresses its various dimensions—social, economic, cultural and legal. It involves promoting equality, fostering economic development, building social harmony, investing in education and awareness, enacting legal reforms and encouraging grassroots initiatives. A collective commitment from individuals, communities, institutions and the government is crucial for creating a more inclusive and just society.

4

Corruption

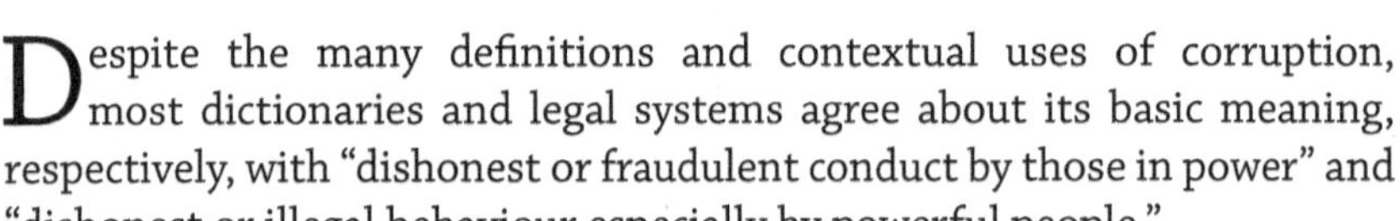

Despite the many definitions and contextual uses of corruption, most dictionaries and legal systems agree about its basic meaning, respectively, with "dishonest or fraudulent conduct by those in power" and "dishonest or illegal behaviour especially by powerful people."

Moving in unison, they then proceed to deeper notions. First comes a transformation from purity to debasement – for example, "a departure from the original or from what is pure or correct."

Second, and relatedly comes the archaic meaning of "decay", "putrefaction" and "decomposition." The Latin words "corruptiō" and "corrumpere" are even clearer on what this transformational process of decay signals, as they are often associated with the words "destroy" or "destruction" in English.

Hence, deep down, corruption refers to the sort of decay that leads to destruction.

5

What is Corruption and why should we care?

Bribery and abuses always occurred, of course. But by the fourth and fifth centuries they had become the norm: no longer abuses of a system, but an alternative system in itself. The cash nexus overrode all other ties. Everything was bought and sold: public office ... access to authority on every level and particularly the emperor. The traditional web of obligations became a marketplace of power, ruled only by naked self-interest. The government's operation was permanently, massively distorted.

Corruption, therefore, ranges in its manifestations from bribery and fraud to socio-political transformations of the greatest magnitude. Corruption, however, does not always lead to collapse. At times, corruption may be better conceived as a sub-optimal way of getting things done when ethically superior ways are perceived as being unavailable, flawed or too costly. Short of collapse, corruption can lead to a tenacious pattern of unethical behaviour that is sustained and replicated over many years. This multiplicity of understandings suggests that corruption is a polyvalent concept. Naturally, it covers a variety of actions by a variety of actors in a variety of contexts. More importantly, from a definitional standpoint, different observers will characterize the same instance of corruption in different ways according to a variety of factors, including their values, assumptions, goals, cultures and skill sets.

Accepting that there are different understandings of corruption and rising to this challenge can help us cultivate an integrated and multi-disciplinary understanding of corruption. At the same time, it is important to ask: what kind of conduct could be causally associated with everything from dishonesty to the downfall of an empire or a political system? The law is perhaps the best place to look for concrete definitions of corrupt actions. However, different legal standards also vary in their approach and implementation. Legal standards are known for their technical and complex formulations and for their susceptibility to multiple interpretations at the hands of lawyers and judges. It rather defines specific acts of corruption, and urges State parties to criminalize these acts in their jurisdictions. This decision is in part the outcome of the difficulty of defining corruption. It also derives from the fact that corruption ranges from a <u>single instance of bribery of a low-ranking customs official to the transformation of a democracy into a kleptocracy (i.e. government by corrupt leaders who exploit people and natural resources in order to extend their personal wealth and political power.</u>

This has parallels with other international instruments that address global crimes, such as organized crime and terrorism, where the international community did not agree on a definition of the overarching concept but approached this matter by defining specific acts.

<u>UNCAC article 15 defines bribery as "[t]he promises, offering or giving, to a public official, directly or indirectly, of an undue advantage, for the official himself or herself or another person or entity, in order that the official act or refrain from acting in the exercise of his or her official duties."</u>

UNCAC article 21 applies the same operative language to private sector actors. While this definition can be difficult to digest, the essence of the crime – money or anything else of value exchanged for benefits from political or economic actors – is not difficult to understand. Nor is it difficult to understand the effect of the crime – circumventing lawful procedures by auctioning off political or economic power to the highest bidder. The same goes for <u>embezzlement and misappropriation of property. Beyond the complex legal definition, the bottom line is that someone entrusted with something valuable (such as property, funds or investments) has taken it for him- or herself or routed it to some third party at the expense of others. It is, essentially, a combination of betrayal and theft.</u> UNCAC article 19 defines the offence of abuse of functions. This offence could apply to situations such as patronage (<u>the use of State resources to reward</u>

    WHAT IS TO BE DONE ?

individuals for their electoral support); nepotism (preferential treatment of relatives); cronyism (awarding jobs and other advantages to friends or trusted colleagues); and sextortion (the demand for sexual favours as a form of payment) – all of which undermine independent or democratically representative decision-making and fair and competitive processes in the formation or staffing of governments. Like the crimes of bribery and embezzlement, these forms of corruption are highly destructive of transparency, accountability and the rule of law. That is not only their effect; it is also their object and purpose. For a further discussion of the crimes defined by UNCAC and the corollary obligations of States that are party to the Convention, see Module 12of the UNODC Module Series on Anti-Corruption.

Effects of Corruption

The effects of corruption are wide-ranging. Some of these effects are fairly obvious, while others require explanation. They include:

Undermining the Sustainable Development Goals

Corruption hampers the attainment of the **United Nations Sustainable Development Goals (SDGs).** The SDGs are comprehensive and their susceptibility to be undermined by corruption is unsurprising: it is entirely conceivable that "a better and more sustainable future for all" often runs counter to the interests of a few and can be derailed through many forms of corruption. Under conditions of diminished State capacity, nations fail to eradicate poverty, address hunger, secure good health-care and high quality education for their citizens, guarantee gender equality and other human rights, reduce inequality and so on. Of particular relevance is Goal 16 of the SDGs (or SDG 16), which is titled "Peace, Justice and Strong Institutions" and aims to "promote peaceful and inclusive societies for sustainable development, provide access to justice for all and build effective, accountable and inclusive institutions at all levels." Given the strong causal link between corruption and institutions that are ineffective, unaccountable and exclusive, three targets of SDG 16 - namely 16.4, 16.5 and 16.6 - specifically call for reducing all forms of corruption, strengthening the recovery and return of stolen assets and developing transparent institutions. At the same time, corruption limits the realization of all SDGs in many respects, as the vast sums that are lost to corruption could have been used to improve living standards by increasing access to housing, health, education and water. For example, the **African**

Union estimates that 25% of Africa's gross domestic product (GDP) is lost to corruption (UNODC, 2015). **Aidt** (2010) examines the relationship between corruption and sustainable development and finds that there is a negative correlation between corruption and growth and that corruption can put a country on an unsustainable path in which its capital base is eroded. In addition, the relationship between corruption and sustainable development has repeatedly been emphasized by resolutions adopted by the **Conference of the States Parties** to UNCAC. It thus requires the global community to see corruption as an obstacle to the realization of the SDGs and to step up anti-corruption efforts if we truly desire to achieve the SDGs. The appendix includes an SDG table that briefly explains how corruption relates to each of the 17 SDGs. For each SDG, the table also indicates which Modules of the E4J University Module Series on Anti-Corruption address the relationship between corruption and the specific SDG.

Economic Loss and Inefficiency

Although obtaining exact figures on the economic costs of corruption is difficult, a 2016 report from the **International Monetary Fund** (IMF) estimated the cost of bribery alone to be between $1.5 to $2 trillion per year. This represents a total economic loss of approximately 2% of global GDP. And yet it does not take into account the economic cost of all other forms of corruption. Regarding fraud, money-laundering and tax evasion, for example, the thousands of leaked documents known as the **Mossack Fonseca Papers** (commonly referred to as the Panama Papers) exposed the vast economic implications of offshore entities for many nations and for economic inequality in general. Finally, beyond deadweight economic loss, there is economic inefficiency to consider. When jobs (or contracts) are given to people (or companies) who offer bribes or share a personal connection, this occurs to the detriment of competition. The result is that more qualified candidates and firms are turned down. The more widespread such practices are, the more inefficient the economy becomes. Corruption in developing countries may cause underdevelopment. This can occur when international economic and humanitarian initiatives are derailed as funds disbursed from loans and aid are embezzled or handed out to inferior contractors who have won their bids through corrupt means (kickbacks, bribery, nepotism, etc.). Furthermore, investment in physical capital and human capital is reduced as resources are diverted from their most beneficial use.

Poverty and Inequality

Corruption is generally not the weapon of the weak. In Nigeria, an (in)famous bribery case, involving the international oil company **Shell**, deprived Nigerian people of over $1.1 billion as the money went to corrupt officials instead of to the national budget (Global Witness, 2017). Meanwhile, according to the **World Bank** (2019), more than 50% of the population of the oil-rich country live in extreme poverty. This example shows that as political and economic systems are enlisted in the service of corrupt actors, wealth is redistributed to the least needy sources. Mechanisms such as political representation and economic efficiency are both compromised by self-dealing and secret exchanges. Under conditions of corruption, funding for education, health-care, poverty relief and elections and political parties' operating expenses can become a source of personal enrichment for party officials, bureaucrats and contractors. Social programmes and the redistributive potential of political systems suffer accordingly. A key result of all the instances named above is a state of unequal opportunity in which advantages arise only for those within a corrupt network.

Personal Loss, Intimidation and Inconvenience

When people experience corruption, it is rarely a positive experience. A bribe must be paid to receive medical attention, obtain a building permit, pick up a package or enjoy phone services. A judge rules against a party, not based on the facts of the case, but because the opponent paid a bribe, knows a power broker or comes from the same racial or ethnic background. A person is beaten, detained or subject to a higher fine because he or she refuses to pay a bribe solicited by a police officer. Retirement funds are lost to fraudsters or tied-up in a money-laundering scheme. While the victims of corruption suffer personal loss, intimidation and inconvenience, those who perpetrate corrupt acts and schemes tend to experience personal gain, a sense of superiority and greater convenience -pending enforcement of the law, that is.

Public and Private Sector Dysfunctionality

The cumulative effect of individual corrupt acts is dysfunctionality. Whether offered by the public or private sectors, the quality of goods and services decrease and the process of obtaining them becomes more expensive, time consuming and unfair. If bribes can successfully be offered

<u>to police, doctors and civil servants,</u> then those who are most successful at extracting these funds get ahead to the detriment of more honest colleagues and competitors who may perform better on merit. Moreover, corporations lose the incentive to offer better services and products if they can undermine competitors through obtaining political favours. State-owned enterprises and industries are structured to enrich government officials instead of pursuing innovation and efficiencies. This can lead to the loss of intrinsic motivation within organizations. Workers and managers are demoralized. People begin to doubt the value of hard work and innovation.

Failures in Infrastructure

When a bridge collapsed in Genoa in August 2018, killing at least 39 people, there were many possible causes to consider **(NZ Herald, 2018).** Corruption was not the most obvious one, but subsequent investigations have found that a Mafia-controlled construction company appears to have used "weakened cement" in the building process. It is widely known that the construction industry is a valuable source of profits and a channel for money-laundering operations by the mafia (additional information on organized crime can be found in the **E4J University Module Series on Organized Crime).** Oversight and competition are both undermined in industries and firms plagued by organized corruption. Relatedly, a 2017 report by **Mexicans Against Corruption** and **Impunity** blamed corruption for the collapse of over 40 buildings during the September 2017 earthquake in Mexico city. Land-use and permit laws appear to have been bypassed, ostensibly through bribery, cronyism and influence trading, leading to the presence of fundamentally unsafe buildings around the capital.

Rigged Economic and Political Systems

What is described as dysfunctional above is actually functional and profitable for corrupt factors. Whether falling under the label of political cronyism, crony capitalism, political party cartels, oligarchy, plutocracy and even kleptocracy, widespread patterns of private and public corruption construct social systems that are rigged in the private interest. Citizens with strong ethical principles (and citizens who lack significant funds, connections, favours to dispense, "hard power" over others such as guns or private enforcers) lose representation, influence and power.

     WHAT IS TO BE DONE ?

Impunity and Partial justice

When corruption pervades the justice system, people can no longer count on prosecutors and judges to do their jobs. The powerful may escape justice. And citizens, especially those with few resources or few powerful allies, may be unfairly accused of crimes, deprived of due process and wrongly imprisoned. Resources on preventing corruption and strengthening integrity in the judiciary are available on the website of the **UNODC Global Judicial Integrity Network.**

Rising Illiberal Populism

A 2017 TI report and several scholarly publications make the point that increasing authoritarianism is partly fuelled by corruption (see, e.g., this post from 2017 by **Balisacan** as well as the resources referenced in this TI paper.) In a nutshell, corruption increases inequality, decreases popular accountability and political responsiveness and thus produces rising frustration and hardship among citizens, who are then more likely to accept (or even demand) hard-handed and illiberal tactics. Those tactics shift the blame for economic insecurity and political decline onto immigrants or other minority groups and onto economic and political elites, who must, the theory goes, be dealt with swiftly and decisively. The rule of law and liberal values of tolerance and human dignity then become obstacles to needed change.

Organized Crime and Terrorism

Nefarious elements in society thrive as proceeds can be laundered, funding disguised and judicial officials and politicians corrupted through bribes (including gifts, favours and other benefits). Levels of violence, illegal drugs, prostitution, sexual slavery, kidnapping and intimidation rise accordingly. The causal arrow goes in both directions. Not only does organized crime cause corruption, but opportunities for corruption left open by a weak, negligent or incapable State can also lead to organized crime.

Diminished State Capacity

Even if citizens were to adamantly demand that the problems listed above be addressed, corruption undermines the power of politics. For example, to the extent that bribery, trading in influence and state capture are widespread, political systems become incapable of addressing social problems whose resolution would threaten vested interests. Naturally, this is never acknowledged as such from within - state incapacity may manifest in a great many distracting and misleading ways, such as wedge issues, political party restructuring, the emergence of scandals and overwhelming outside issues that detract from structural problems and so on. Under conditions of state capture, political arbitrage can be expected to occur in a highly strategic fashion. Issues will be played off against each other in order to frustrate systemic reforms. Moreover, as **Della Porta** and **Vannucci** (2005) argue, corruption compromises the ethos of public service and changes political culture so as to render meaningful, public-spirited reforms virtually unthinkable.

Increasing Polarization and Unrest

When corruption, in particular state capture, becomes the norm, this can lead to polarization among citizens: those in support of corrupt regimes (because of kickbacks and handouts) versus those opposed to them. In the presence of diametrically opposed groups in society, compromise and reasoned discussion diminish. Policy is judged not on the basis of ideology or a project's inherent merits, but on who the policy proponents are and what benefits competing networks can reap.

Climate Change and Damage to Biodiversity

Corruption derails anti-climate change funding and initiatives, defeats forest conservation and sustainable forest management programmes and fuels wildlife and fishery crimes (for more information, see the **E4J University Module Series on Wildlife, Forest** and **Fisheries Crime).** These and other adverse effects of corruption on climate change and the environment are underscored in a TI report from 2011 and additional TI publications. On a broader level, the book, **This Changes Everything** by Naomi Klein (2014) details how state capture by monied interests has derailed legislative efforts to address climate change in the United States. Her analysis applies to many countries around the world, given the power of the fossil fuels and automotive industries over governments - elected and unelected - across the globe. The perilous impact of corruption on the fisheries sector is discussed in detail in the publication **Rotten Fish** (UNODC, 2019), while the report **Authorized to Steal** (CIEL, 2019) reveals how corruption enables criminal networks to illegally harvest timber in Peru.

Human Rights Violations

The observation that corrupt rulers tend to view civil liberties as obstacles to the consolidation of power can be traced back to many historical sources, including the collection of eighteenth century essays on corruption and tyranny known as **Cato's Letters.** Most recently of all, perhaps, the **United Nations Office of the High Commission for Human Rights** (OHCHR) has noted significant connections between corruption and human rights violations. Not only do those who report and oppose corruption end up on the receiving end of assassinations and human rights violations of many kinds, but also corruption itself decreases the States capacity to address violations of civil and political rights and to make the necessary provisions to guarantee such rights, including socio-economic rights, which often require complex initiatives on the part of governments. OHCHR calls corruption "a structural obstacle to the enjoyment of human rights" and has detailed many intersections between these two areas.

Armed Conflict and Atrocity Crimes

The diminished States capacity and development, brought about by corruption, can lead to insecurity and even armed conflict (see, e.g., **World Bank, 2011; World Bank, 2017)**. Indeed, corruption has been recognized as a destabilizing factor and ultimately a "driver of conflict" **(USIP, 2010, p. 7)**. Although the causal link between corruption and atrocity crimes (including genocide, war crimes and crimes against humanity) may be hard to prove, transitional justice mechanisms have identified corruption as a root cause of conflict and atrocity. See, for example the **Sierra Leone Truth** and **Reconciliation Commission Report (2004, chap. 2, para. 13)** and the **Liberian Truth and Reconciliation Commission Consolidated Final Report (2009, vol. II, pp. 16-17)**. In post-Arab Spring Tunisia, corruption was recognized as a root cause of the conflict even before the transitional justice mechanism operated. Thus, **Tunisia's Law on Transitional Justice** from 2013 and the **Truth and Dignity Commission** that was created by the law were intended to establish accountability for the country's legacy of rampant corruption and human rights violations and to help reform the institutions that engaged in such crimes. Another relevant example is a 2018 report from the **Open Society Justice Initiative**, which offers evidence linking corruption to crimes against humanity in Mexico.

Public Frustration and Cynicism

People lose trust in leaders, in social systems (public institutions) and sometimes even in society and ethics itself when they sense that corruption is widespread and corrupt actors are not being held accountable. When political non-accountability increases, such perceptions persist for protracted periods and political participation diminishes. Moreover, public frustration and the sense that corruption is widespread can in turn pave the way for citizens themselves to take part in corrupt transactions, as discussed in a post on the **Taxi Driver Paradox.** In other words, social norms could encourage corrupt behaviour as people tend to think that "if everybody is doing it, I might as well do it too." **(Köbis, 2018).** Failure to meet public expectations for zero-tolerance of corruption may have deleterious consequences for the legitimacy of State institutions and the very utility of formal norms that citizens and firms are expected to follow, possibly resulting in higher public tolerance of un-civic and free-riding behaviour.

6

The Duties of every Indian Citizen towards Himself

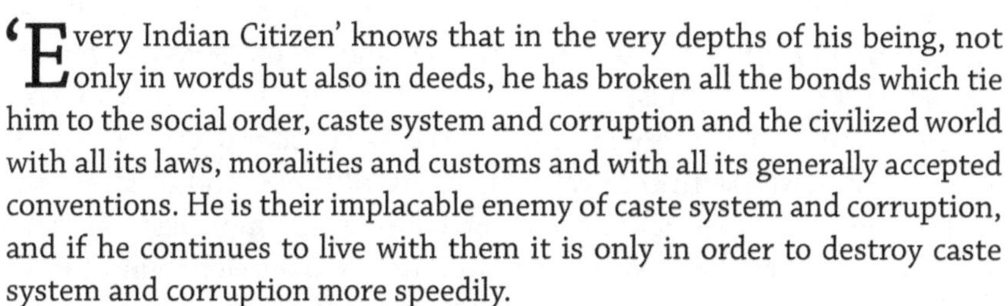

'Every Indian Citizen' knows that in the very depths of his being, not only in words but also in deeds, he has broken all the bonds which tie him to the social order, caste system and corruption and the civilized world with all its laws, moralities and customs and with all its generally accepted conventions. He is their implacable enemy of caste system and corruption, and if he continues to live with them it is only in order to destroy caste system and corruption more speedily.

'Every Indian Citizen' despises all doctrines and refuses to accept the mundane sciences, leaving them for future generations. He knows only one science: the science of destruction of caste system and corruption. For this reason, but only for this reason, he will study mechanics, physics, chemistry, and perhaps medicine. But all day and all night he studies the vital science of human beings, their characteristics and circumstances', and all the phenomena of the present social order caste system and corruption. The object is perpetually the same: the surest and quickest way of destroying the whole filthy order and people involved in corruption.

'Every Indian Citizen' should despise public opinion. He despises and hates the existing social morality, caste system and corrupt social order, in all its manifestations. For him, morality is everything which contributes to the triumph of India and revolution. Immoral and criminal is everything that stands in its way.

'Every Indian citizen' is a dedicated person, merciless towards the caste system and corruption, corrupt officials, corrupt politicians and toward the corrupt classes; and he can expect no mercy from them. Between him and them there exists, declared or concealed, a relentless and irreconcilable war to death. He must accustom himself to torture.

Tyrannical towards himself, he must be tyrannical towards others. All the gentle and enervating sentiments of kinship, love, friendship, gratitude and even honour, must be suppressed in him and give place to the cold and single-minded passion for India and revolution. For him, there exists only one pleasure, one consolation, one reward, one satisfaction – the success of the revolution and our country. Night and day he must have but one thought, one aim – merciless destruction of caste system and corruption and people who are involved in it. Striving cold-bloodedly and indefatigably toward this end.

The nature of the true 'Every Indian Citizen' should exclude all sentimentality, romanticism, infatuation and exaltation. All private hatred and revenge must also be excluded. 'Every Indian Citizen's' passion, practiced at every moment of the day until it becomes a habit, is to be employed with cold calculation. At all times, and in all places, 'Every Indian Citizen' must obey not his personal impulses, but only those which serve the cause of the revolution and development of India and destruction of caste system and corruption (and people involved in corruption)

The Relations of every Indian Citizen towards his Comrades

'Every Indian Citizen' can have no friendship or attachment, except for those who have proved by their actions that they, like him, are dedicated to revolution and the destruction of caste system and corruption. The degree of friendship, devotion and obligation toward such a comrade is determined solely by the degree of his usefulness to the cause.

The Relations of every Indian Citizen towards Society

The new member, having given proof of his loyalty not by words but by deeds, can be received into the society only by the unanimous agreement of all the members.

'Every Indian Citizen' enters the world of the State, of the privileged classes, of the so-called civilization and he lives in this world only for the purpose of bringing about its speedy and total destruction of caste system and corruption along with the people involved in it. He is not an 'Indian Citizen' if he has any sympathy for this caste system and corruption and people who are involved in it. **He should not hesitate to destroy any position, any place or any man who is corrupt in this world. He must hate everyone and everything in it with an equal hatred. He is no longer anIndian Citizen if he is swayed by these relationships with corrupt system and corrupt politicians.**

This filthy social order and corrupt politicians can be split up into several categories. The first category comprises those who must be condemned to death without delay. Comrades should compile a list of those to be condemned **(CORRUPT Government officials, Corrupt Ministers and their families along with their associates,Corrupt Politicians and Corrupt Media)** according to the relative gravity of their crimes; and the constitutional executions should be carried out according to the prepared order.

The second group comprises **(Small time Contractors, PIMPs, Confidants, Family and Associates of these CORRUPT Bastards)** those who will be spared for the time being in order that, by a series of monstrous acts.

The third category consists of a great many brutes in high positions, distinguished neither by their cleverness nor their energy, while enjoying riches, influence, power and high positions by virtue of their rank. These must be exploited in every possible way; they must be implicated and embroiled in our affairs, their dirty secrets must be ferreted out and they must be transformed into slaves. Their power, influence and connections, their wealth and their energy, will form an inexhaustible treasure and a precious help in all our undertaking of destruction of caste system and corruption.

The fourth category comprises ambitious office-holders and liberals of various shades of opinion. 'Every Indian Citizen' must pretend to collaborate with them, blindly following them, while at the same time, prying out their secrets until they are completely in his power. They must be so compromised that there is no way out for them.

The fifth category consists of those doctrinaires, conspirators and revolutionists who cut a great figure on paper or in their cliques. They must be constantly driven on to make compromising declarations: as a result, the majority of them will be destroyed, while a minority will become genuine revolutionaries.

The Attitude of the Society towards the People

The Society has no aim other than the complete liberation and happiness of the masses – i.e., of the people who live by manual labour. Convinced that their emancipation and the achievement of this happiness can only come about as a result of an all-destroying popular revolt, the Society will use all its resources and energy towards increasing and intensifying the evils and miseries of the people until at last their patience is exhausted and they are driven to a general uprising.

With this end in view, the Society, therefore, refuses to impose any new organization from above. Any future organization will doubtlessly work its way through the movement and life of the people; but this is a matter for future generations to decide. Our task is terrible, total, universal and merciless destruction of caste system and corruption.

Therefore, in drawing closer to the people, we must above all make common cause with those elements of the masses which, since the foundation of the country of India, have never ceased to protest, not only in words but in deeds, against everything directly or indirectly connected with the state: against the social order, the bureaucracy, the clergy, the traders and the parasitic middlemen. We must unite with the adventurous people who have similar ideologies, who are the only genuine revolutionaries in India.

To weld the people into one single unconquerable and all-destructive force to destroy caste system and corruption along with the people who are involved in it – this is our aim, our conspiracy, and our task.

7

Attitude towards Sex and its Education

Sex Education in the Netherlands

by Anisha Abraham | Children, Education, Health

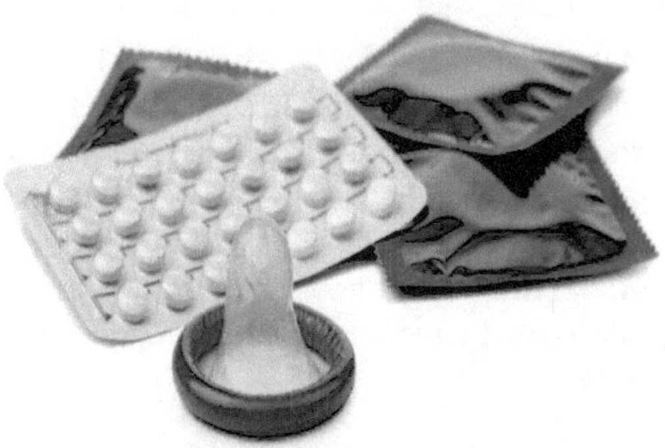

What is the Dutch attitude to sex education and what will your child be taught in school? Pediatrician Anisha Abraham outlines the curriculum in the Netherlands and offers advice about approaching this subject with your children.

Let's talk about Sex: Dutch style

How many of you have visited the Nemo Science Museum? A visit to the 3rd floor is a clear indication that the Dutch have an open view about sex education. There visitors can find an exhibit geared towards teens entitled **'Let's talk about sex.'** Displays in this exhibit include the science of sexual attraction, the French kiss, the many forms of contraception, and mannequins in various sexual positions. For some, this level of openness may be a bit shocking. For the Dutch, it's part of a concerted effort to start the discussion about sex early and make it a normal part of growing-up.

A Healthy Attitude

The Dutch may very well be on to something. According to Dutch foundation Rutgers, a sexual research institute, Dutch youth have the lowest teen pregnancy rates in Europe. Dutch kids receive sex education earlier and choose to have sex later than other European teens. In fact, the average age for their first sexual intercourse is 17, a year older than in Britain. What's more, teen sexual encounters in the Netherlands are generally viewed as positive/wanted and enjoyable, whereas in the United States, nearly 2/3 of sexually-active teens surveyed said they wished they had waited longer to have sex. Research also shows that the majority of young people in the Netherlands use some form of protection when having sex and have relatively low rates of HIV infection and sexually-transmitted diseases.

Early Intervention

What do the Dutch do differently? Dutch parents tend to openly discuss sex and their adolescents' romantic or sexual relationships. Moreover, sex education starts early in the Netherlands. By age four, youngsters discuss their bodies in class. By the teenage years, formal sex education focuses on having positive relationships, negotiating with partners and using contraception. This differs vastly from other countries, where the pervasive attitude is more conservative and significant taboos around discussing sex exist.

Applying the Rutgers Philosophy to the Dutch Curriculum

Not only do the Dutch start to teach sex education early, they also make sex education mandatory. Since 2012, age-appropriate sex education – including gender identity issues – is compulsory in all Dutch schools. **Rutgers** is the organization behind much of the Netherlands sex education curriculum. Ineke van der Vlugt, an expert on youth sexual development, explains on the institution's website that, for teens, sexuality is about self-image, developing their own identity, gender roles and learning to find their boundaries. Rutgers' sex education is geared to help young people make well-informed choicesand has been adopted by a number of local and international schools in the Netherlands. Their materials use direct, age-appropriate language and simple images.

Rutgers' Spring Fever curriculum starts at age 4-5 discussing feelings, being a boy versus a girl, etc. At age 7, sessions include discussing respect and attraction, and at age 8-9 same sex attractions (i.e. some of you may have two mommies). By age 10-11, topics include changes during puberty, love and datingand men and women in the media. The **'Long Live Love'** (Lang leve de liefde) curriculum aims to give teenagers the skills to make their own decisions and focuses not only on the biological aspects of reproduction but also values, attitudes, communication and negotiation skills. A big focus of the Rutgers message is on feeling positive and having open communication.

Shing Chan is a school teacher who leads the sexuality education classes at a primary school in central Amsterdam. According to Shing, her school curriculum is very much based on the needs of the students. When leading sessions for students ages 8-11 years, their focus is on changes that occur during puberty, such as having periods and acknowledging feelings and attractions. Classes are conducted separately for boys and girls and are done in small groups, several times per year. Classes may incorporate educational TV clips/video segments and generally allow for classroom discussion. Parents are told at the beginning of the year which issues will be discussed, but are not typically notified before each sexuality education session.

Discrepancies Despite its successes, not everyone is entirely happy with this approach. A few parents interviewed for this article felt that they did not know what exactly was being taught, when and how much their child actually knew. Although mandatory, actual information can vary, teachers may not receive specific training and the classes are not standardized.

In addition, according to the government, nearly 1/2 of the children in Amsterdam are from non-western backgrounds. Given the increased diversity of religious and cultural backgrounds, there are wide differences in views on sexuality and gender identity. Because of that, according to Shing, depending on the school and location, certain subjects such as gender identity may be presented differently or less openly at the primary school level. Still, there is no denying that the Dutch sex education is stronger and more open than in most other countries. Dutch sex education supports the philosophy that topics like masturbation, homosexuality and sexual pleasure are normal and natural.

So what's the bottom line for parents and kids? Sex education is comprehensive in the Netherlands. However, parents should be encouraged to discuss topics at home and keep the lines of communication open. There is strong evidence that children whose parents discuss sex with them are more likely to delay having sex, use contraception and have fewer partners.

How can parents help educate their children?

As a paediatrician, here are a few tips that I have compiled from healthychildren.org and have used in my clinical practice:

1. Don't wait for your kids to be teens to have a conversation. Start early, use every-day opportunities and have an active, ongoing dialogue with your child.

2. Keep the subjects appropriate such as discussing good touch/bad touch or the names of body parts with kids ages 4-5 years and progressing to more detailed discussions about positive relationships and handling pressure to be sexually active as your child gets older.

3. Use correct terms. Using nicknames for your child's sexual anatomy may relay the message that these body parts should not be talked about or are embarrassing, so avoid this.

4. Reassure your child that kids mature at different rates. Explain what happens during puberty, including bodily changes and sexual attraction.

5. Children often worry whether they're normal. Remind them that you love them and that they are special.

6. Continue to remind teens that it's OK to wait and there are other ways to express affection. Factors such as curiosity and peer pressure often drive young people to have sex.

7. When having conversations, ask about peer group or friends first and use open-ended questions. For example: "What do your friends think about the sex-ed class at school?" "Is anyone dating?" before progressing to more personal questions such as: "What do you think of sex-ed class?" and "Do you feel pressure to have sex?"

8. Finally, reinforce self-esteem. Tell children that they are unique. Discuss how healthy relationships should be based on trust and love and reinforce that saying "no" means "no."

　　　　WHAT IS TO BE DONE ?

8

The Struggle of the Urban Workers

Many farmers have probably heard about the labour unrest in the towns. Some of them have themselves been in the capitals and in the factories, and have seen the riots, as the police call them. Others must have seen the leaflets issued by the workers or pamphlets about the workers' struggle. Still others have only heard stories about what is going on in the towns from people with first-hand experience.

Formerly, only students rebelled, but now thousands and tens of thousands of workers have risen in all the big towns. In most cases they fight against their employers, against the factory owner sand against the capitalists. The workers declare strikes, stop work at a factory, at the same time demand higher wage sand at the same time demand that they should be made to work not eleven or ten hours a day, but only eight hours. The workers also demand other things that would make the working man's life easier. They want the workshops to be in better condition and the machines to be protected by special devices so as to prevent them from maiming the workers; they want their children to be able to go to school and the sick to be given proper aid in the hospitals; they want the workers' homes to be like human dwellings instead of being like pigsties.

The police intervene in the workers' struggle. They seize workers, throw them into prison and deport them without trial to jail. The government has passed laws banning strikes and workers' meetings. But the workers wage their fight against the police and against the government. The workers say: "We, millions of working people, have bent our backs long enough! We have worked for the rich and remained paupers long enough! We have allowed them to rob us long enough! We want to unite in unions, to unite all the workers in one big workers' union (a workers' party) and to strive jointly for a better life. We want to achieve a new and better order of society: <u>in this new and better society there must be neither rich nor poor; all will have to work. Not a handful of rich people, but all the working people must enjoy the fruits of their common labour.</u> Machines and other improvements must serve to ease the work of all and not to enable a few to grow rich at the expense of millions and tens of millions of people." This new and better society is called **socialist society.** The teachings about this society are called **socialism**. The workers' unions which fight for this better order of society are called **Social-Democratic** parties. Such parties exist openly in nearly all the countries, and our workers, together with socialists from among the educated people, have also formed such a party,CPI, CPI(M). CPI(lM).

The government persecutes that party, despite all prohibitions; it publishes its newspapers and pamphlets and organises secret unions. The workers not only meet in secret but come out into the streets in crowds and unfurl their banners bearing the inscriptions: <u>"Long live the eight-hour day! Long live freedom! Long live socialism!"</u> The government savagely persecutes the workers for this. It even sends troops to shoot down the workers. Soldiers have killed workers in Delhi, Punjab and Haryana.

But the workers do not yield. They continue the fight. They say: neither persecution, prison, deportation, penal servitude, nor death can frighten us. <u>Our cause is a just one. We are fighting for the freedom and the happiness of all who work. We are fighting to free tens and hundreds of millions of people from abuse of power, oppression and poverty. The workers are becoming more and more class-conscious.</u> The number of Social-Democrats is growing fast in all countries. We shall win despite all persecution.

The rural poor must clearly understand who these Social-Democrats are, what they want and what must be done in the villages to help the Social-Democrats win happiness for the people.

What do the Social-Democrats want?

The Karnataka Social-Democrats are the first and foremost striving to win **political liberty**. They need political liberty in order to unite all the Karnataka workers extensively and openly in the struggle for a new and better socialist order of society.

What is Political liberty?

To understand this, the labourer should first compare his present state of freedom with bonded labour. Under the farmer-owning system, the bonded labour could not marry without the landlord's permission. Today, the bonded labour is free to marry without anyone's permission. Under the bonded labour system, the farmer had unfailingly to work for his landlord on days fixed by the latter's bailiff. Today, the labourer is free to decide which employer to work for, on which days and for what pay. Under the bonded labour system, the labour could not leave his village without the landlord's permission. Today, the labour is free to go wherever he pleases—if the **landlord** allows him to go, if he is not in arrears with his taxes, if he can get a passport and if the Governor or the police chief does not forbid his changing residence. Thus, even today, the labourer is not quite free to go where he pleases; he does not enjoy complete freedom of movement; the labourer is still a semi- bonded labour. Later on, we shall explain in detail why the

Indian labourer is still semi-bonded and what must he do to escape from this condition.

Under the bonded labour system, the bonded labour had no right to acquire property without the landlord's permission; he could not buy land. Today, the bonded labour is free to acquire any kind of property (but even today he is not quite free to leave the landlord; Thanks to BR Ambedkar. he is not quite free to dispose of his land as he pleases). Under the bonded labour system, the labourer could be flogged by order of the landlord. Today, the peasant cannot be flogged by order of the landlord, although he is still liable to corporal punishment.

This <u>freedom is called **civil** liberty</u>—freedom in family matters, in private matter sand in matters concerning property. The labourer and the workers are free (although not quite) to arrange their family life and their private affairs, to dispose of their labour (choose their employer) and their property.

But neither the Karnataka workers nor the Karnataka people as a whole are yet free to arrange their **public** affairs. The people as a whole are the bonded labourer of the government officials, just as the labourers were the bonded labourer of the landlords. The Karnataka people have no right to choose their officials, no right to elect representatives to legislate for the whole country. The Karnataka people have not even the right to arrange meetings for the discussion of **state** affairs. We dare not even print newspapers or books and dare not even speak to all and for all on matters concerning the whole state without permission from officials who have been put in authority over us without our consent, just as the landlord used to appoint his bailiff without the consent of the labourers!

Just as the labourers were the slaves of the landlords, so the Karnataka people are still the slaves of the officials. Just as the labourers lacked civil freedom under the labourer-owning system, so the Karnataka people still lack **political** liberty. <u>Political liberty means the freedom of the people to arrange their public, state affairs. Political liberty means the right of the people to elect their representatives toState Elections (VidhanaSouda). All laws should be discussed and passed, all taxes should be fixed only by such State Elections (VidhanaSouda),elected by the people themselves: not by buying out the voters with alcohol and money. Political liberty means the right of the people themselves to choose all their officials, arrange all kinds of meetings for the discussion of all state affairs and publish whatever papers and books they please, without having to ask for permission.</u>

 What Is To Be Done ?

All the other European people won political liberty for themselves long ago. Only in Pakistan, in India and other 3rd world countries are the people still politically enslaved by the dictator's government and by the autocratic government. Autocracy means the unlimited power of the PRIME MINISTER. The people have no voice in determining the structure of the state or in running it. All laws are made and all officials are appointed by the PRIME MINISTER alone, by his personal, unlimited, autocratic authority. But, of course, the PRIME MINISTER **cannot even** know all Indian laws and all Indian officials. The PRIME MINISTER cannot even know all that goes on in the country. The PRIME MINISTER simply endorses the will of a few score of the richest and most high-born officials. However much he may desire to, one man cannot govern a vast country like India. It is not the PRIME MINISTER who governs India—it is only a manner of speech to talk about autocratic, one-man rule! India is governed by a handful of the richest and most high-born officials. The PRIME MINISTER learns only what this handful are pleased to tell him. The PRIME MINISTER cannot in any way go against the will of this handful of high-ranking BJP-RSS members: the PRIME MINISTER himself is a RSS member and a member of the BJP-RSS Fascist group; since his earliest childhood he has lived only among these high-born people; it was they who brought him up and educated him; he knows about the Karnataka people as a whole only that which is known to these noble gentry, these rich landlords, and the very few rich merchants who are received at the PRIME MINISTER's court.

In every administration office, you will find the same picture hanging on the wall; it depicts the PRIME MINISTER speaking to the headmen who have come to his coronation. "Obey your Marshals of the RSS!" the PRIME MINISTER is ordering them. And the present PRIME MINISTER, Narendra Modi, has repeated those words. Thus, the PRIME MINISTER's themselves admit that they can govern the country only with the aid of RSS and through the BJP. We must well remember those words of the PRIME MINISTER's about the labourers having to obey the RSS. We must clearly understand what lies is being told to the people by those who try to make out that the PRIME MINISTER's government is the best form of government. In other countries—those people say—the government is elected; but it is the rich who are elected and they govern unjustly and oppress the poor. In Karnataka, the government is not elected; an autocratic PRIME MINISTER governs the whole country. The PRIME MINISTER stands above everyone, rich and poor. The PRIME MINISTER, they tell us, is just to everyone, to the poor and to the rich alike.

Such talk is sheer hypocrisy. Every Indian knows the kind of justice that is dispensed by our government. Everybody knows whether a plain worker or a farm labourer in our country can become a member of the State Council. In all other Asian countries, however; they have been able to speak freely to all the people about the miserable condition of the workers, and call upon the workers to unite and fight for a better life. And no one has dared to stop these speeches of the people's representatives; no policeman has dared to lay a finger on them.

In Karnataka there is no people elective government, (it is being influenced by money, caste, religion and alcohol) and she is governed not merely by the rich and the high-born, but by the worst of these. She is governed by the most skilful intriguers at the PRIME MINISTER's court, by the most artful tricksters, by those who carry lies and slanders to the PRIME MINISTER and flatter and toady to him. They govern in secret; the people do not and cannot know what new laws are being drafted, what wars are being hatched, what new taxes are being introduced, which officials are being rewarded and for what services and which are being dismissed. In no country, is there such a multitude of officials as in India. <u>These officials tower above the voiceless people like a dark forest</u>—a mere worker can never make his way through this forest, can never obtain justice. <u>Not a single complaint against bribery, robbery or abuse of power on the part of the officials is ever brought to light; every complaint is smothered in official red tape.</u> The voice of the individual never reaches the whole people, but is lost in this dark jungle, stifled in the police torture chamber. An army of officials, <u>who were never elected by the people and who are not responsible to the people, has woven a thick web and men and women are struggling in this web like flies.</u>

The PRIME MINISTER's autocracy is an autocracy of officials. The PRIME MINISTER's autocracy means the feudal dependence of the people upon the officials and especially upon the police. The PRIME MINISTER's autocracy is police autocracy.

That is why the workers come out into the streets with banners bearing the inscriptions: <u>"Down with autocracy!", "Long live political liberty!"</u> That is why tens of millions of the rural poor must also support and take up this battle-cry of the urban workers. Like them, undaunted by persecution, fearless of the enemy's threats and violence and undeterred by the first reverses, the agricultural labourers and the poor labourers must come forward for a decisive struggle for the freedom of the whole of the Karnataka people and demand first of all the **convocation of the representatives of the people**. Let the people themselves all over Karnataka elect their representatives. Let those representatives form a supreme assembly, which will introduce elective government in Karnataka, free the people from feudal dependence upon the officials and the police and secure for the people the right to meet freely, speak freely and have a free press!

That is what the Social-Democrats want first and foremost. That is the meaning of their first demand: the **demand for political liberty**.

We know that political liberty, free elections to the State Assembly, freedom of assembly, freedom of the press, will not at once deliver the working people from poverty and oppression. There is no means of immediately delivering the poor of town and country from the burden of working for the rich. <u>The working people have no one to place their hopes in and no one to rely upon, **but themselves.** Nobody will free the working man from poverty **if he does not free himself**. And to free themselves the workers of the whole country</u>, the whole of Karnataka, must unite in one union, in one party. But millions of workers cannot unite if the autocratic police government bans all meetings, all workers' newspapers and the election of workers' deputies. To unite they must have the right to form unions of every kind, must have freedom to unite; they must enjoy political liberty.

Political liberty will not at once deliver the working people from poverty, but it will give the workers a weapon with which to fight poverty. There is no other means and there can be no other means of fighting poverty except the **unity of the workers themselves**. But millions of people cannot unite unless there is **political liberty.**

In all other Asian countries where the people have won political liberty, the workers began to unite long ago. Throughout the whole of Asia, workers who own no land and no workshops, and work for other people for wages all their lives are called **poor**. Over fifty years ago, the call was sounded for the working people to unite. "Workers of all countries, unite!"—during the past fifty years these words have circled the whole globe, are repeated at tens and hundreds of thousands of workers' meetings, and can be read in millions of Social-Democratic pamphlets and newspapers in every language.

Of course, to unite millions of workers in one union, in one party, is an extremely difficult task; it requires time, persistence, perseverance and courage. <u>The workers are ground down by poverty and want, benumbed by ceaseless toil for the capitalists and landlords; often they have not even the time to think of why they remain perpetual paupers or how to be delivered from this. Everything is done to prevent the workers from uniting: either by means of direct and brutal violence,</u> as in countries like India where there is no political liberty or by refusing to employ workers who preach the doctrines of socialism, or, lastly, by means of deceit and bribery. <u>But no violence or persecution can stop the poor workers from fighting for the great cause of the emancipation of all working people from poverty and oppression</u>. The number of Social-Democratic workers is constantly growing. Take Australia; there they have elective government. Formerly, in Australia, too, there was an unlimited, autocratic, monarchist government. But long ago, over fifty years ago, the Australian people destroyed the autocracy and won political liberty by force. In Australia, laws are not made by a handful of officials, as in India, but by an **assembly of people's representatives,** by a parliament. All adult males take part in electing deputies to this assembly. This makes it possible to count how many votes were cast for the Social-Democrats. Among the farm labourers of Karnataka, socialism is not yet widespread but it is now making very rapid progress among them. And when the masses of farm-hands, day labourers and poor, pauperised labourers unite with their brothers in the towns, the Karnataka workers will win and establish an order under which the working people will suffer neither poverty nor oppression.

By what means do the Social-Democratic workers want to deliver the people from poverty?

To know this, one must clearly understand the cause of the poverty of the vast masses of the people under the present social order. Rich cities are growing, magnificent shops and <u>houses are being built, railways are being constructed, all kinds of machines and improvements are being introduced in industry and agriculture, but millions of people remain in poverty and continue to work all their lives to provide a bare subsistence for their families. That is not all: more and more people are becoming unemployed. Both in town and country there are more and more people who can find no work at all.</u> In the villages they starve, while in the towns they swell the ranks of the "tramps" and "down-and-outs," find refuge like beasts in dug-outs on the outskirts of towns or in dreadful slums and cellars, such as those in the Kalasipalya market in Bengaluru.

Why is this happening? Wealth and luxury are increasing and yet the millions and millions who by their labour create all this wealth remain in poverty and want! Labourers are dying of starvation, workers wander about without employment and yet merchants export millions of pounds of grain from Karnataka to foreign countries, factories are standing idle because the goods cannot be sold, for there is no market for them!

The cause of all this, first of all is, that most of the land and also the factories, workshops, machines, buildings, ships, etc., belong to a small number of rich people. Tens of millions of people work on this land and at these factories and workshops, but they are all owned by a few thousand or tens of thousands of rich people, landlords, merchants and factory owners. The people work for those rich men for hire, for wages, for a crust of bread. All that is produced over and above to provide a bare subsistence for the workers goes to the rich; this is their profit, their "income." All the benefits arising from the use of machines and from improvements in methods of production go to the landowners and capitalists: they accumulate wealth untold, while the workers get only a miserable pittance. The workers are brought together for work; on large estates and at big factories several hundred and sometimes even several thousand workers are employed. When labour is united in this way and when the most diverse kinds of machines are employed, work becomes more productive: one worker produces much more than scores of workers did working separately and without the aid of machines. But the benefits of this productive labour goes not to all the working people, but to an insignificant number of big landowners, merchants, and factory owners.

One often hears it said that the landlords and merchants "provide work" for the people, that they "provide" the poor with earnings. It is said, for instance, that a neighbouring factory or a neighbouring landlord "maintains" the local labourers. Actually, however, the workers by their labour **maintain** themselves and also all those who do not work themselves. But **for permission** to work on the landlord's land, at a factory or on a railway, the worker **gives** the owner all he produces, while the worker himself gets only enough for a bare subsistence. Actually, therefore, it is not the landlords and the merchants who give the workers employment, but the workers who by their labour maintain everybody, surrendering the greater part of their labour.

Further, in all present-day states the people's poverty is due to the fact that the workers produce all sorts of articles for sale, for the market. The factory owner and the artisan, the landlord and the well-to-do labourer produce various goods, raise cattle, sow and harvest grain **for sale**, in order to obtain **money**. Money has everywhere become the ruling power. All the goods produced by human labour are exchanged for money. With money you can buy anything. With money you can even buy a man, that is to say, force a man who owns nothing to work for another who has money. Formerly, land used to be the ruling power—that was the case under the labourer-owning system: whoever possessed land possessed power and authority. Today, however, money and capital, has become the ruling power. With money, you can buy as much land as you like. Without money, you will not be able to do much even if you have land: you must have money to buy a plough or other implements, to buy livestock, to buy clothes and other town-made goods, not to speak of paying taxes. For the sake of money, nearly all the landlords have mortgaged their estates to the banks. To get money, the government borrows from rich people and bankers all over the world and pays hundreds of crores of rupees yearly in interest on these loans.

For the sake of money, everyone today is waging a fierce war against everyone else. Each tries to buy cheap and to sell dear, each tries to get ahead of the other, to sell as many goods as possible, to undercut the other, to conceal from him a profitable market or a profitable contract. In this general scramble for money the little man, the petty artisan or the small labourer, fares worse than all: he is always left behind by the rich merchant or the rich labourer. The little man never has any reserves; he lives from hand to mouth; each difficulty or accident compels him to pawn his last belongings or to sell his livestock at a trifling price. Once he has fallen into the clutches of a middlemen or of a pawn broker he very rarely succeeds in escaping from the net and in most cases he is utterly ruined. Every year tens and hundreds of thousands of small labourers and artisans lock up their cottages, surrender their holdings to the commune and become wage-workers, farm-hands, unskilled worker sand poor. But the rich grows richer and richer in this struggle for money. They pile up millions and hundreds of millions of rupees in the banks and make profit not only with their own money, but also with the money deposited in the banks by others. The little man who deposits a few score or a few thousand rupees in a bank or a savings-bank receives interest at the rate of three or four paisa to the rupee; but the rich makes millions out of these scores and use these millions to increase their turnover and make ten and twenty paisa to the rupee.

   WHAT IS TO BE DONE ?

That is why the Social-Democratic workers say that the only way to put an end to the poverty of the people is to change the existing order from top to bottom, throughout the country, and to establish **a socialist order**, in other words, to take the estates from the big landowners, the factories from the factory owners, and money capital from the bankers, to abolish their **private property which is worth more than 100 crores** and turn it over to the whole working people throughout the country. When that is done, the workers' labour will be made use of not by rich people living on the labour of others, but by the workers themselves and by those elected by them. The fruits of common labour and the advantages from all improvements and machinery will then benefit all the working people and all the workers. Wealth will then grow at a still faster rate because the workers will work better for themselves than they did for the capitalists; the working day will be shorter; the workers' standard of living will be higher; and all their conditions of life will be completely changed.

But it is not an easy matter to change the existing order throughout the country. That requires a great deal of effort, a long and stubborn struggle. All the rich, all the property-owners, all the Rich will defend their riches with all their might. The officials and the army will rise to defend all the **rich class**, because the government itself is in the hands of the rich class. The workers must rally as one man for the struggle against all those who live on the labour of others; the workers themselves must unite and help to unite all the poor in a single **working class**, in a **single poor class**. The struggle will not be easy for the working class, but it will certainly end in the workers' victory because the Rich, or those who live on the labour of others, are an insignificant minority of the population, while the working class is the vast majority. The workers against the property-owners means millions against thousands.

The workers in Karnataka are already beginning to unite for this great struggle in a single workers' Social-Democratic Party. Difficult as it is to unite in secret, hiding from the police, nevertheless, the organisation is growing and gaining strength. When the Karnataka people have won political liberty, the work of uniting the working class, the cause of socialism, will advance much more rapidly, more rapidly than it is advancing among the Karnataka workers.

10

Riches and Poverty, Property-Owners and Workers in the Villages

We know now what the Social-Democrats want. They want to fight with the rich class and to free the people from poverty. In our villages there is no less and, perhaps, even more poverty than there is in the towns. We shall not speak here about how great the poverty in the villagesis. Every worker who has been in the country and every labourer are well acquainted with want, hunger and ruin in the villages.

But the labourer does not know the **cause** of his distress, hunger and destitution or **how** to rid himself of this want. To know this, one must first find out what causes all want and poverty in both town and villages. We have already dealt with this briefly and we have seen that the poor peasants and rural workers must unite with the urban workers. But that is not enough. We must also find out what sort of people in the villages will follow the rich, the property-owners and what sort of people will follow the workers, the Social-Democrats. We must find out whether there are many labourers who, no less than the landlords, are able to acquire capital and live on the labour of others. Unless we get to the bottom of this matter, no amount of talking about poverty will be of any use and the rural poor will not know **who** in the villages must unite among themselves and with the urban workers, or **what** must be done to make it a **dependable** union and

<u>to prevent the labourer from being hoodwinked by his own kind, the rich labourer, as well as by the landlord.</u>

To get to the bottom of this, let us now see how strong the landlords are and how strong the rich labourers are in the villages.

Let us begin with the landlords. We can judge of their strength in the first place by the amount of land they own as private property. A total of **123,100 km² of land** is cultivated in Karnataka constituting 64.6% of the total geographical area of the state. The total amount of land in Karnataka, including labourer allotment land and privately owned land, has been calculated at about 40,000,000 acres (except the state lands, of which we shall speak separately). Out of this total of 40,000,000 acres, 31,000,000 acres of allotment land are held by the labourers, that is to say, by **over ten million households;** whereas 09,000,000acres are held by private owners, i.e., by **less than half a million families.** Thus, even if we take the average, every labourer family holds 13 acres, while every family of private owners owns 218 acres! But the distribution of land is much more unequal, as we shall presently see.

Of the 09,000,000 acres owned by private owners, **seven** million are **zamindaris**, in other words, the private property of the members of the imperial family. The PRIME MINISTER, with his capitalist, is the first landlord, the biggest landowner in Karnataka. **One** family possesses more land than **half a million** labourer families! Further, the temples, mosques, churches and monasteries own about one million acres of land. Our priests preach frugality and abstinence to the labourers, but they themselves have, by fair means and foul, accumulated an enormous amount of land.

Further, about two million acres are owned by the cities and towns and an equal amount by various commercial and industrial companies and corporations two million acres(the exact figure is 1,605,845, but to simplify matters we will quote round figures) belong to **less than half a million** (81,358) families of private owners. Half these families are quite small owners, owning less than ten acres of land each, and all of them together own less than one million acres. On the other hand, **sixteen thousand** families own **over one thousand** acres each; and the total land owned by them amounts to **five million acres.** What vast areas of land are concentrated in the hands of the big landowners is also to be seen in the fact that **just under one thousand families** (924) own more than ten thousand **acres** each, and all together they own **twenty-seven million**

acres! One thousand families own as much land as is owned by two million labourer families.

<u>Obviously, millions and tens of millions of people are bound to live in poverty and starvation and **will go** on living in poverty and starvation as long as such vast areas of land are owned by a few thousand of the rich. Obviously, the state authorities, the government itself</u> (even the PRIME MINISTER's government) will always dance to the tune of these big landowners. Obviously, the rural poor can expect no help from anyone, or from any quarter, until they unite, combine in a single class to wage a stubborn, desperate struggle against the landlord class.

At this point we must observe that very many people in this country (including even many people of education) have a totally wrong idea about the strength of the landlord class; they say that the "state" owns much more land. These bad counsellors of the labourer say: "A large portion of the territory [i.e., of all the land] of Karnataka already belongs to the state. "The mistake these people make arises from the following. They have heard that the **state** owns 10,000,000 acres of land in Karnataka. That is true. But they forget that these 10,000,000 acres consist almost entirely of **uncultivable land and forests in the far North.** Thus, the state has retained only that land which up to the present has been quite unfit for cultivation. The cultivable land owned by the state amounts to **less than four million acres**. And these cultivable state lands, are leased for very low rents, for next to nothing, to the rich. The rich lease thousands and tens of thousands of acres of these lands and then sublet them to the labourers at exorbitant rents.

The people who say that the state owns a great deal of land are very bad counsellors of the labourer. The actual case is that the big private landowners (including the PRIME MINISTER's associates Adani and Ambani) own a lot of good land, and the state itself is in the hands of these big Capitalists and landowners. As long as the rural poor fail to unite, and by uniting become a formidable force, the "state" will always remain the obedient servant of the landlord class. There is another thing that must not be forgotten: formerly almost all are landlords. The zamindaris still owns a vast amount of land. But today money, capital, has become the ruling power. Merchants and well-to-do labourers have bought very large amounts of land. It is estimated that in the course of thirty years the Capitalist lost (i.e., sold more than they bought) land to the value of over six hundred million rupees. And, merchants and honorary citizens have acquired land to the value of 250,000,000 rupees. Labourers, farmers, and "other rural inhabitants" (as our government calls the common folk, to distinguish them from the "gentry," the "clean public") have acquired land to the value of 300,000,000 rupees. Thus, on the average, every year, the labourers in the whole of Karnataka acquire land as private property to the value of 10,000,000 rupees.

<u>And so, there are different sorts of labourers: some live in poverty and starvation; others grow rich. Consequently, the number of rich labourers who incline towards the landlords and will take the side of the rich against the workers is increasing.</u> The rural poor who want to unite with the urban workers must carefully ponder over this and find out whether there are many rich labourers of this kind, how strong they are, and what kind of a union we need to fight this force. We have just mentioned the bad counsellors of the labourer. Those bad counsellors are fond of saying that the labourers already have such a union. That union is the **Union**, the village commune. The **Union**, they say, is a great force. The **Union** unites the labourers very closely; the organisation (i.e., the association, unity) of the labourers in the **Union** is colossal (i.e., enormous, boundless).

That is wrong. It is a tale. A tale invented by kind-hearted people, but a tale nevertheless. If we listen to tales we shall only wreck our cause, the cause of uniting the rural poor with the urban workers. Let every rural inhabitant look round carefully: is the unity of the **Union**, is the labourer commune, at all like a union of the poor to fight **all** the rich, **all** those who live on the labour of others? No, it is not, and it cannot be. In every village, in every commune, there are many farm labourers, many impoverished labourers and there are rich labourers who employ farm labourers and buy land "in perpetuity." These rich labourers are also members of the commune, and it is they who lord it in the commune because they are a force. But do we need a union to which the rich belong and which is lorded over by the rich? Of course not. We need a union to **fight** the rich. And so, the unity of the **Union** is of no good to us at all.

What we need is a voluntary union, a union only of people who have realised that they must unite with the urban workers. The village commune, however, is not a voluntary union; it is enforced by the state. The village commune does not consist of people who work for the rich and who want to unite to fight for the rich. The village commune consists of all sorts of people, not because they want to be in it, but because their parents lived on the same land and worked for the same landlord and because the authorities have registered them as members of that commune. The poor labourers are not free to leave the commune; they are not free to accept in the commune a man whom the police have registered in another region, but whom we may need for our union in a particular village. No, we need a very different kind of union, a voluntary union consisting only of labourers and poor labourers to fight all those who live on the labour of others.

The times when the **Union** was a force have long passed, never to return. The **Union** was a force when hardly any of the labourers were farm labourers, or workers wandering over the length and breadth of Karnataka in search of a job, when there were hardly any rich labourers, when all were equally ground down by the feudal landlords. But now money has become the principal power. Members of the same commune will now fight one another for money like wild beasts. The moneyed labourers sometimes oppress and fleece their fellow labourers more than the landlords do. What we need today is not the unity of the **Union**, but a union against the **power of money**, against the rule of capital, a union of all the rural labourers and of all the poor labourers of different communes, a union of all the rural poor with the urban workers to fight both the landlords and the rich labourers.

We have seen how strong the landlords are. We must now see whether there are many rich labourers and how strong they are.

The rich labourers not only buy land in perpetuity; most often they take land for a number of years, on lease. By renting large plots they prevent the rural poor from getting land. For example, it has been calculated how much land rich labourers have rented in Karnataka alone. And what do we find? The number who rented thirty acres or more per household is very small, only two out of every fifteen households. But these rich labourers have gained possession of **one half** of all the rented land and each of them has on the average **seventy-five acres** of the rented land! Or take Mandya, where a calculation has been made of how much of the land rented by the labourers from the state through the **Union**, through the village commune, has been grabbed by the rich. It has been found that the rich, who account for only **one-fifth** of the total number of households, have grabbed **three-fourths** of the rented land. Everywhere land goes to those who have money and only the few rich have money.

Further, much land is now let by the labourers themselves. The labourers abandon their holdings because they have no livestock, no seed, nothing with which to run their farms. Today, even land is of no use unless you have money. For instance, sometimes even two, out of every three rich labourer house-holds **rent allotment land** in their own or in another commune. The allotments are let by those who have no cows, or only one cow. **One-fourth** of the labourer allotments, a quarter of a million acres, are let. Of this quarter of a million acres, one hundred and fifty thousand acres (three-fifths) are rented by rich labourers! This, too, shows whether the unity of the **Union**, the commune, is of any use to the poor. In the village commune, he who has money has power. What we need is the unity of the poor of all communes.

Just as with land purchase, the labourers are deceived by talk about buying cheap ploughs, harvesters and all sorts of improved implements. Improved implements will better the conditions of the labourers. That is mere deception. All these improved implements always go to the rich; the poor get next to nothing. They cannot think of buying ploughs and harvesters; they have enough to do to keep body and soul together!

Finally, one of the main features of the rich labourers is that they **hire farm-hands** and **day labourers**. Like the landlords, the rich labourers also live on the labour of others. Like the landlords, they grow rich because the mass of the labourers are ruined and pauperised. Like the landlords, they try to squeeze as much work as they can out of their farm-hands and pay them as little as possible. If millions of labourers were not utterly ruined and compelled to go to work for others, become hired labourers, sell their labour-power—the rich labourers could not exist, could not carry on their farms. There would be no "abandoned" allotments for them to pick up and no labourers for them to hire. The million and a half rich labourers throughout Karnataka certainly hire no less than a **million** farm-hands and day labourers. Obviously, in the great struggle between the propertied class and the class of the property less, between masters and workers, between the rich and the poor, the rich labourers will take the side of the property-owners against the working class.

We now know the position and the strength of the rich labourers. Let us examine the conditions of the rural poor.

We have already said that the rural poor comprise the vast majority, almost two-thirds, of the labourer households throughout Karnataka. To begin with, the number of households without cows cannot be less than **three million—probably** more than that today, perhaps three and a half million. Every famine year, every crop failure, ruins tens of thousands of farms. The population grows, life on the land becomes more crowded, but all the best land has been grabbed by the landlords and the rich labourers. And so, every year more and more people are ruined, go to the towns and the factories, take work as farm-hands, or become unskilled labourers. A labourer who has no cow is one who has become quite poor. <u>He gains a living (if you can call it living; it would be truer to say that he just contrives to keep body and soul together) not from the land, not from his farm, but</u> **by working for hire**. He is brother to the town worker. Even land is of no use to the labourer without a cow: half the households without cows **let their allotments**, while some even surrender them to the commune for nothing (and sometimes even pay the difference between the taxes and the expected income from the land!) because they are not in a position to till their land. A labourer who has no cow sows one acre or two at the most. He always has to buy additional grain (if he has the money to buy it with)— his own crop will never suffice to feed him. Labourers who own one cow each and there are about three and a half million such households throughout Karnataka, which are not very much better off. Of course, there are exceptions, and we have already said that, here and there, there are labourers with one cow each who are doing middling well or are even rich. But we are not speaking of exceptions, of individual localities, but of Karnataka as a whole. If we take the entire mass of labourers who have one cow each, there can be no doubt that they are a mass of paupers. Even in the agricultural davangere the labourer who has one cows cows only three or four acres, rarely five; his crop does not suffice either. Even in a good year his food is no better than that of a labourer without a cow—<u>which means that he is always underfed, always starves. His farm is in decay, his livestock is poor and short of fodder and he is not in a position to look after his land properly.</u> The labourer who owns one cow—in Dharwad, for instance—can afford to spend (not counting expenditure on fodder) not more than **twenty thousand rupees a** year on the whole of his farm! (A rich labourer spends **ten times as much**.) Twenty thousand rupees a year for rent, to buy livestock, repair his wooden plough and other implements, pay the shepherd, and for everything else! Do you call that farming? It is sheer misery, hard labour and endless drudgery. It is natural that some of the labourers with one cow each, and not a few, should also **let their allotments**. Even land is of little use to a pauper. He has no money and his land does not even provide him with enough to eat, let alone with money. But money is needed for everything: for food, for clothing, for the farm and to pay taxes. In Shivamogga, a labourer who owns one cow usually has to pay **about eighteen hundred rupees** a year in taxes alone, while he

     What Is To Be Done ?

cannot make more than seventy-five thousand rupees a year to meet **all** his expenses. Under these circumstances, it is sheer mockery to talk about buying land, about improved implements, about agricultural banks: those things were not invented for the poor.

Where canthe labour rerget the money from? He has to look for "earnings" on the side. A labourer who owns one cow, like the labourer who owns none, ekes out a living only with the help of "earnings." But what does "earnings" mean? It means working for others, working for hire. It means that the labourer who owns one cow has half-ceased to be an independent farmer and has become a hireling, a poor farmer. That is why such labourers are called semi-poor. They, too, are brothers to the town workers because they, too, are fleeced in every way by all sorts of employers. They, too, have no way out, no salvation, except by uniting with the Social-Democrats to fight all the rich, all the property-owners. Who works on the building of railways? Who is fleeced by the contractors? Who goes out lumbering and timber-floating? Who works as farm-hand? Or as day labourer? Who does the unskilled work in the towns and ports? It is always the rural poor, the labourers who have no cows or only one each. It is always the rural poor and semi-poor. And what vast numbers of these there are in Karnataka! It has been calculated that throughout Karnataka eight and sometimes even nine **lakhs people** are taken out yearly. Those are all for migratory workers. They are labourers only in name; actually, they are hirelings, wage-labourers. They must all unite in one union with the town workers—and every ray of light and knowledge that reaches the villages will strengthen and consolidate this unity.

There is one more point about "earnings" that must not be forgotten. All kinds of officials and people who think as the officials do are fond of saying that the labourer, the poor, "needs" two things: land (but not very much of it— besides, he cannot get much, because the rich have grabbed it all!) and "earnings." Therefore, they say, in order to help the people, it is necessary to introduce more trades in the rural districts, to "provide" more "earnings." Such talk is sheer hypocrisy. For the poor, "earnings" mean wage-labour. To "provide earnings" for the labourer means transforming him into a wage-labourer. Fine sort of assistance this! For the rich labourers there are other kinds of "earnings," which require capital, for instance, the building of a flour-mill or some other plant, the purchase of threshing-machines, trade and so on. To confuse the earnings of moneyed people with the **wage-labour** of the poor means deceiving the poor. Of course, this deception is to the advantage of the rich; it is to their advantage to make it appear that all kinds of "earnings" are open to and within the reach of **all** the labourers. But he who really cares for the welfare of the poor will tell **the whole truth and nothing but the truth.**

It remains for us to consider the middle labourers. We have already seen that, on the average, taking Karnataka as a whole, we must regard as a middle labourer one who has a pair of draught animals and that too out of a total of ten million households there are about two million middle class farmer households in Karnataka. The middle labourer stands between the rich labourer and the poor, and that is why he is called a middle labourer. His standard of living, too, is middling: in a good year he makes ends meet on his farm, but poverty is always knocking at his door. He has either very few savings or none at all. That is why his farm is in a precarious position. He finds it hard to get money: only very seldom can he make as much money out of his farm as he needs, and if he does, it is just barely enough. To go out for earnings would mean neglecting the farm and everything would go to rack and ruin. Nevertheless, many of the middle labourers cannot get along without earnings: they, too, have to hire themselves to others; want compels them to go into bondage to the landlord, to fall into debt. And once in debt, the middle labourer is hardly ever able to get out of it, for unlike the rich labourer he has no steady income. Therefore, once he falls into debt it is as if he had put his neck in a halter. He remains a debtor until he is utterly ruined. It is chiefly the middle labourer who falls into bondage to the landlord, because for work paid on a job basis the landlord needs a labourer who is not ruined, one who owns a pair of cows and all implements required in farming. It is not easy for the middle class farmer to go elsewhere in search of earnings, so he goes into bondage to the landlord in return for grain, permission to use pasture land, the lease of the cut-off lands, and money advances during the winter. The middle labourer is hard pressed, not only by the landlord and the middleman also, but also by his rich neighbour, who is always one jump ahead when he wants to acquire more land and never misses an opportunity to squeeze him in some way or the other. Such is the life of the middle labourer; he is neither fish nor fowl. He can be neither a real master nor a worker. All the middle labourers strive to become masters: they want to be property-owners, but very few succeed. There are a few, a very few, who even hire farm-hands or day labourers, try to become rich on the labour of others, to rise to wealth on the backs of others. But most middle labourers have no money to hire labourers— in fact, they have to hire themselves out.

      WHAT IS TO BE DONE ?

Whenever a struggle begins between the rich and the poor, between the property-owners and the workers, the middle labourer remains in between, not knowing which side to take. The rich call him to their side: you, too, are a master, a man of property, they say to him, you have nothing to do with the penniless workers. But the workers say: the rich will cheat and fleece you and there is no other salvation for you but to help us in our fight against all the rich. This struggle for the middle labourer is going on everywhere, in all countries, wherever the Social-Democratic workers are fighting to emancipate the working people. In Karnataka, the struggle is just beginning. That is why we must most carefully study the matter and understand clearly the deceits the rich resort to in order to win over the middle labourer; we must learn how to expose these deceits and help the middle labourer to find his real friends. If the Karnataka Social-Democratic workers at once take the right road, we shall establish a firm alliance between the rural workers and the urban workers more quickly than our comrades, the Indian workers, and we shall speedily achieve victory over all the enemies of the working people.

11

What path should the Middle Labourer take? Should he take the side of the Property-Owners and the Rich or the side of the Workers and the Poor?

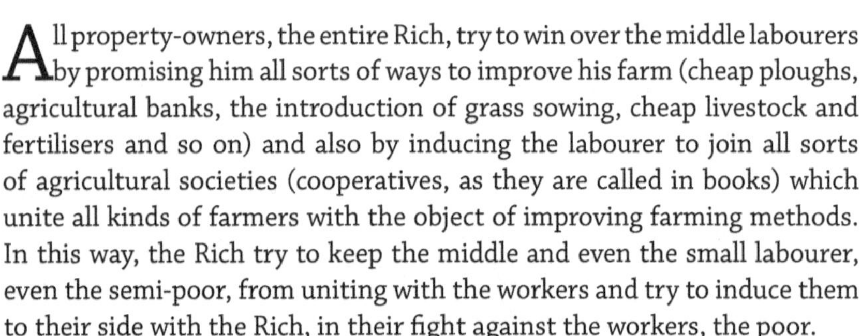

All property-owners, the entire Rich, try to win over the middle labourers by promising him all sorts of ways to improve his farm (cheap ploughs, agricultural banks, the introduction of grass sowing, cheap livestock and fertilisers and so on) and also by inducing the labourer to join all sorts of agricultural societies (cooperatives, as they are called in books) which unite all kinds of farmers with the object of improving farming methods. In this way, the Rich try to keep the middle and even the small labourer, even the semi-poor, from uniting with the workers and try to induce them to their side with the Rich, in their fight against the workers, the poor.

To this the Social-Democratic workers reply: improved farming is an excellent thing. There is no harm in buying cheaper ploughs; nowadays even a merchant, if he is not a fool, tries to sell more cheaply to attract customers. But when a poor or a middle labourer is told that improved farming and cheaper ploughs will help all of them to escape from poverty and to get on their feet, without touching the rich, **this is deception**. All these improvements, lower prices and cooperatives (societies for the sale

     What Is To Be Done ?

and purchase of goods) **benefit the rich far more than anybody else.**
The rich grow stronger and oppress the poor and middle labourers more
and more. As long as the rich remains rich, as long as they own most of the
land, livestock, implements and money—as long as all this lasts, not only
the poor but even the middle labourers will **never** be able to escape from
want. One or two middle labourers may be able to climb into the ranks of
the rich with the aid of all these improvements and cooperatives, but the
people as a whole, and all the middle labourers, will sink deeper and deeper
into poverty. For **all** middle labourers to become rich, the rich themselves
must be turned out and they can be turned out only if the urban workers
and the rural poor are united.

The Rich say to the middle (and even to the small) labourer: we will sell
you land at a low price, and ploughs at a low price, but in return you must
sell yourselves to us and give up fighting all the rich.

The Social-Democratic worker says: if you are really offered goods at a low
price, why not buy them, if you have the money; that is sound business. But
you should never sell yourselves. To give up the fight in alliance with the
urban workers against the entire Rich would mean remaining in poverty
and want forever. If goods become cheaper, the rich will gain still more and
become richer. But those who never have money to spare will gain nothing
from cheaper goods until they take that money from the Rich.

Let us take an example. Those who support the Rich make much ado about
all sorts of cooperatives (societies for buying cheap and selling profitably).
There are even people who call themselves "Socialist-Revolutionaries,"
who, echoing the Rich, also talk loudly about the labourer needing nothing
so much as cooperatives. All sorts of cooperatives are beginning to spring
up in Karnataka, too, although there are still a very few of them here, and
there will not be many until we enjoy political liberty. Take Telangana:
there the labourers have many cooperatives of all kinds. But see who gains
most from these cooperatives. In all Telangana, 140,000 farmers belong to
societies for the sale of milk and dairy products, and these 140,000 farmers
(we again take round figures for the sake of simplicity) own 140,000 cows.
It is calculated that there are **four million** poor labourers in Telangana.
Of these, only 40,000 belong to cooperatives: thus, **only one** out of every
hundred poor labourers enjoys the benefits of these cooperatives. These
40,000 poor labourers own only 100,000 cows in all. Further, the middle
farmers, the middle labourers, number **one million**; of these, 50,000
belong to cooperatives (that is to say, five out of every hundred) and they

own a total of 200,000 cows. Finally, the rich farmers (i.e., both landlords and rich labourers) number **one-third of a million**; of these, 50,000 belong to cooperatives (that is to say, **seventeen** out of every hundred!) and they own 800,000 cows!

That is whom the cooperatives help first and foremost. That is how the labourer is deceived by those people who talk loudly about saving the middle labourer by means of such societies for buying cheap and selling profitably. It is, indeed, at a very low price that the Rich want to "buy off" the labourer from the Social-Democrats, who call upon both the poor and the middle labourer to join them.

In our State, too, cooperative cheese dairies and amalgamated dairies are beginning to be formed. In our state, too, there are plenty of people who shout: the **Union**, and cooperatives—that is what the labourer needs. But see who gains by these cooperatives and renting by the **Union**. <u>Out of every hundred households in our country, at least twenty own no cows at all; thirty own only one cow each: these sell milk from dire need, their own children have to go without milk, starve and die off like flies. The rich labourers, however, own three, four and more cows each, and these rich labourers own half the total number of cows owned by labourers. Who, then, gains from cooperative cheese dairies?</u> Obviously, the landlords and the labourer Rich gain first of all. Obviously, it is **to their advantage** that the middle labourers and the poor should follow in their wake and that they should believe that the means of escaping from want is not the struggle of all the workers against the entire Rich, but the striving of individual small farmers to climb out of their present position and get into the ranks of the rich.

This striving is fostered and encouraged in every way by all the champions of the Rich, who pretend to be the champions and friends of the small labourer. And <u>many simple-minded people fail to see the wolf in sheep's clothing </u>and repeat this rich deception in the belief that they are helping the poor and middle labourers. For instance, they argue in books and in speeches that small-scale farming is the most profitable, most remunerative form of farming, that small-scale farming is flourishing, and that is why, they say, there are so many small producers in agriculture everywhere, and why they cling to their land (and not because all the best lands are owned by the Rich and all the money, too, while the poor have to live in drudgery all their lives crowded on tiny patches of land!). The small labourer does not need much money, these smooth-tongued people say; the small and the middle labourers are thriftier and more industrious than the big farmers, and know how to live a simpler life; instead of buying hay for their cattle, they are content to feed them on straw. Instead of buying an expensive machine, they get up earlier and toil longer and do as much as a machine does; instead of paying money to strangers for doing repairs, the labourer himself takes his hatchet on a Sunday and does a bit of carpentry—and that is much cheaper than the way a big farmer goes about it; instead of feeding an expensive cow or an ox, he uses his cow for ploughing. In Telangana, all the poor labourers use cows to haul their ploughs, and in our state, too, the people have become so impoverished that they are beginning to use not only cows, but men and women to pull ploughs! How profitable, how cheap all this is! How praiseworthy of the middle and small labourers to be so industrious, so diligent, to live such simple lives, and not to waste their time on nonsense, not to think of socialism, but only of their farms, not to strive towards the workers who organise strikes against the Rich, but towards the rich and try to join the ranks of respectable folk! If only all were so industrious and so diligent and lived frugally and did not drink and saved more money and spent less on clothes and had fewer children—all would be happy and there would be no poverty and no want!

Such are the sweet songs the Rich sings to the middle labourer and there are simpletons who believe these songs and repeat them! Actually, all these honeyed words are nothing but deceit and mockery of the labourer. What these smooth-tongued people call cheap and profitable farming is the want, the dire need, which forces the middle and small labourers to work from morning till night, to begrudge himself a crust of bread, to grudge every penny he spends. Of course, what can be "cheaper" and "more profitable" than to wear the same pair of trousers for three years, go about barefoot in summer, repair one's wooden plough with a piece of rope, and feed one's cow on rotten straw from the roof! Put a Rich or a rich labourer on such a "cheap" and "profitable" farm, and he will soon forget all this honeyed talk!

The people who extol small-scale farming sometimes want to help the labourer, but actually they only do him harm. With their honeyed words they deceive the labourer in the same way as people are deceived by a **lottery**. I shall tell you what a lottery is. Let us suppose I have a cow, worth 50 thousand. I want to sell the cow by means of a lottery, so I offer everyone tickets at a thousand each. Everyone has a chance of getting the cow for one thousand! People are tempted and thousands pour in. When I have collected a hundred thousand, I proceed to draw the lottery: the one whose ticket is drawn gets the cow for a thousand, the others get nothing. Was the cow "cheap" for these people? No, it was very dear, because the total money they paid was double the value of the cow, because two persons (the one who ran the lottery and the one who won the cow) gained without doing any work and gained at the expense of the ninety-nine who lost their money. Thus, those who say that lotteries are advantageous to the people are simply practising deceit on the people. Those who promise to deliver the labourers from poverty and want by means of cooperatives of every kind (societies for buying cheap and selling profitably), improved farming, banks and all that sort of thing, are deceiving them in exactly the same way. Just as in a lottery where there is one winner and all the rest are losers, so it is with these things: one middle labourer may manage to get rich, but ninety-nine of his fellow labourers bend their backs all their lives, never escape from want, and even sink more deeply into poverty. Let every villager examine his commune and the whole district a little more closely: are there many middle labourers who become rich and forget want? And how many are there who can never rid themselves of want? How many are ruined and leave their villages? As we have seen, it has been calculated that in the whole of Karnataka there are not more than two million middle labourer farms. Suppose there were ten times as many societies of all kinds for buying cheap and selling profitably as there are now. What would the result be? It would be a big figure if a hundred thousand middle labourers succeeded in raising themselves to the level of the rich. What would that mean? It would mean that out of every hundred middle labourers, five would become rich. But what about the other ninety-five? They would be in the same straits as ever and many of them would be in even greater difficulties and the poor would only be impoverished all the more!

Of course, the Rich want nothing more than that the largest possible number of middle and small labourers should strive to get rich, **believe** in the possibility of escaping from poverty without fighting the Rich, place their **hopes** in diligence and frugality and in becoming rich and not in uniting with the rural and urban workers. The Rich do all they can to foster this deceptive faith and hope in the labourer and try to lull him with honeyed words.

To expose the deception practised by these smooth-tongued people it is sufficient to ask them three questions.

Question one: Can the working people rid themselves of want and poverty when, in Karnataka, a fifty million acres out of twenty million acres of arable land belong to private landowners? When sixteen thousand very big landowners possess twenty million acres?

Question two: Can the working people rid themselves of want and poverty when one and a half million rich labourer households (out of a total of ten million) have concentrated in their hands half of all labourers' land under crops, half the total number of cows and livestock owned by labourers and much more than half the total labourer stocks and savings? When this labourer Rich is growing richer and richer, oppressing the poor and middle labourers, making money out of the labour of others, of the farm-hands and day labourers? When six and a half million households consist of poor labourers, destitute, always starving and reduced to winning a miserable crust of bread by all kinds of wage-labour?

Question three: Can the working people rid themselves of want and poverty when money has become the ruling power, when everything can be bought for money—factories and land and even men and women can be bought to serve as wage-workers, wage-slaves? When no one can live or run a farm without money? When the small farmer, the poor labourer, has to wage a struggle against the big farmer to get money? When a few thousand landlords, merchants, factory owners and bankers have concentrated in their hands hundreds of millions of rupees, and, moreover, control all the banks, where thousands of millions of rupees are deposited?

No honeyed words about the advantages of small-scale farming or of cooperatives will enable you to evade these questions. To these questions there can be only one answer: the real "cooperation" that can save the working people is the **union** of the rural poor with the Social-Democratic workers in the towns to fight the entire Rich. The faster **this** union grows and becomes strong, the sooner will the middle labourer realise that the promises of the Rich are all lies, and the sooner will the middle labourer come over to our side.

The Rich know this, and that is why, in addition to honeyed words, they spread all sorts of lies about the Social-Democrats. They say that the Social-Democrats want to deprive the middle and small labourers of their property. **That is a lie.** The Social-Democrats want to deprive of their property only the big proprietors, **only those who live on the labour of others.** The Social-Democrats **will never take away the property of the small and middle farmers who do not hire labourers.** The Social-

Democrats defend and champion the interests of all the working people, not only the interests of the urban workers, who are more class-conscious and more united than the others, but also of the agricultural workers and of those small artisans and labourers who do not hire workers, do not strive towards the rich and do not go over to the side of the Rich. **The Social-Democrats are fighting for all improvements in the conditions of the workers and labourers** which can be introduced immediately, when we have not yet destroyed the rule of the Rich and which will help them in the struggle against the Rich. But the Social-Democrats do not deceive the labourer; they tell him **the whole truth**, plainly tell him in advance that no improvements will rid the people of want and poverty as long as the Rich is in power. To enable **all the people** to know what the Social-Democrats are and what they want, the Social-Democrats have drawn up a programme. A programme is a brief, clear and precise statement **of all the things a party is striving and fighting for.** The Social-Democratic Party is the only party that advances a clear and precise programme for all the people to know and see and for the party to consist only of people who really want to fight for the emancipation of all the working people from the yoke of the Rich, and who properly understand who must unite for this fight and how the fight must be conducted. Furthermore, the Social-Democrats believe that they must **explain** in their programme, in a direct, frank and precise way, **the causes of the poverty and want among the working people** and why the unity of the workers is becoming wider and stronger. It is not enough to say that life is hard and to call for revolt; every tub-thumper can do that, but it is of little use. The working people must clearly understand **why** they are living in such poverty and **with whom they must unite** in order to fight to liberate themselves from want.

We have already stated what the Social-Democrats want; we have explained the causes of the working people's want and poverty; we have indicated whom the rural poor must fight and with whom they must unite for this fight.

We shall now explain **what improvements** we can win **at once** by fighting for them, improvements in the lives of the workers and in the lives of the labourers.

12

What improvements are the Social-Democrats striving to obtain for the Whole People and for the Workers?

The Social-Democrats are fighting for the liberation of all the working people from all robbery, oppression and injustice. To become free, the working class must first of all become united. And to become united it must have freedom to unite, have the right to unite and have **political liberty.** We have already said that autocratic government means enslavement of the people by the officials and the police. Political liberty is, therefore, needed by the whole people, except a handful of courtiers and a few money-bags and high dignitaries who are received at court. But most of all, political liberty is needed by the workers and the labourers. The rich can escape the self-will and the tyranny of officials and the police by buying them off. The rich can make their complaints heard in the highest places. That is why the police and the officials take much fewer liberties with the rich than with the poor. The workers and the labourers have no money to buy off the police or the officials; they have no one to complain to and are not in a position to sue them in court. The workers and the labourers will never rid themselves of the extortions, tyranny and insults of the police and the officials as long as there is no **elective government** and as long as there is no **national assembly of MPs.** Only such a national assembly of MPs can free the people from enslavement by the officials. Every intelligent labourer must support the Social-Democrats, who first and foremost demand of the PRIME MINISTER's government **the convocation of a national assembly of MPs.** The representatives must be elected by all, irrespective of social-estate or irrespective of wealth or poverty. The elections must be free, without any interference on the part of the officials; they must be carried out under the supervision of such that enjoy the people's confidence, and not of police officers or the tahsildar. Under such conditions, MLAs representing the entire people will be able to discuss all the needs of the people and introduce a better state of affairs in Karnataka.

The Social-Democrats demand that officials must be severely punished for arbitrarily arresting anyone. To put an end to their self-assumed power, they must be chosen by the people and everyone must have the right to lodge a complaint against any official directly in a court. What is the use of complaining to the tahsildar about a police officer, or to the Governor about the tahsildar? The tahsildar will, of course, always protect the police officer and the Governor will always protect the tahsildar, while the complainant will get into trouble. He runs a fair chance of being put into prison. The officials will be curbed only, when everyone in Karnataka (as in all other states) has the right to complain both to the national assembly and to the elected courts and to speak freely of his needs and to write about them in the newspapers.

The Social-Democrats demand that the social-estates be abolished and that all the citizens of the state enjoy exactly the same rights. Today, the social-estates are divided into tax-paying and non-tax-paying, into privileged and non-privileged; we have blue blood and common blood; even the birch has been retained for the common people. In no other country are the workers and labourers in such a position of inferiority. In no country, except India, are there different laws for different social-estates. It is time the Karnataka people, too, demanded that every labourer should possess **all the rights** possessed by the RICH. Is it not a disgrace that the birch should still be used and that a tax paying social-estate should still be in existencein more than 75 years of Independence?

Feudal system thinks the peasant will not hear what he is saying and will not understand. Why allow people to go away when the landlords need cheap labour? <u>The more crowded the people are on the land the more that is to the landlords' advantage; the poorer the labourers are, the more cheaply can they be hired and the more meekly will they submit to oppression of every kind.</u>

What Is To Be Done ?

The Social-Democrats demand that the standing army be neutralised and use army for developmentaland first responders workand that a militia be established in its stead, that all the people be armed. A standing army is an army that is divorced from the people and trained to shoot down the people. <u>If the soldier were not locked up for years in barracks and inhumanly drilled there, would he ever agree to shoot down his brothers, the workers and the labourers? Would he go against the starving labourers? A standing army is not needed in the least to protect the country from attack by an enemy;</u> a people's militia is sufficient. If every citizen is armed, Karnataka need fear no enemy. And the people would be relieved of the yoke of the military clique. The upkeep of this clique costs **hundreds of millions of rupees a year,** and all this money is collected from the people; that is why the taxes are so heavy and that is why it becomes increasingly difficult to live. The military clique still further increases the power of the officials and police over the people. This clique is needed to plunder foreign people, for instance, to take the land from the Australian. This does not ease but, on the contrary, increases the people's burden because of greater taxation. The substitution of the armed nation for the standing army would enormously ease the burden of all the workers and all the labourers.

Similarly, **the abolition of indirect taxation**, which the Social-Democrats demand, would be an enormous relief. Indirect taxes are such taxes that are not imposed directly on land or on a house but are paid by the people **indirectly**, in the form of higher prices for what they buy. The state imposes taxes on sugar, alcohol, petrol, matches and all sorts of articles of consumption; these taxes are paid to the Treasury by the merchant or by the manufacturer, but, of course, he does not pay it out of his own pocket, but out of the money his customers pay him. The price of alcohol, sugar, petrol and matches goes up and every purchaser of a bottle of alcohol or of a pound of sugar has to pay the tax in addition to the price of the goods. For instance, if, say, you pay hundred for a kilo of sugar, 40 rupees (approximately) constitute the tax: the sugar-manufacturer has already paid the tax to the government and is now exacting from every customer the sum he has paid. Thus, indirect taxes are taxes on articles of consumption, taxes which are paid by the purchaser in the form of higher prices for the articles he buys. It is sometimes said that indirect taxation is the fairest form of taxation: you pay according to the amount you buy. But this is not true. Indirect taxation is the most unfair form of taxation, because it is harder for the poor to pay indirect taxes than it is for the rich. The richman's income is ten times or even a hundred times as large as that of the labourer or worker. But does the rich man need a hundred times as much sugar? Or ten times as much alcohol or matches or petrol? Of course not! A rich family will buy twice, at most, three times as much petrol, alcohol or sugar as a poor family. But that means that the rich man will pay **a smaller part** of his income in taxes than the poor man. Let us suppose that the poor labourer's income is twenty thousand rupees a year; let us suppose he buys 6000 rupees worth of such goods as are taxed and which are consequently dearer (the tax on sugar, matches, petrol, is an **excise duty**, i.e., the manufacturer pays the duty before placing the goods on the market; in the case of alcohol, a state monopoly, the State simply raises the price; cotton goods, iron and other goods have risen in price because cheap foreign goods are not admitted into Karnataka unless a heavy duty is paid on them). Of these 6000rupees, **2000 rupees** will constitute the tax. Thus, out of every rupee of his income the poor farmer will pay **ten paisa** in indirect taxes (exclusive of direct taxes, land redemption payments, quit-rent, land tax, and Union taxes). The rich labourer has an income of 1 lakh rupees; he will buy one thousand and fifty rupees' worth of taxed goods and pay **200 rupee** in taxes (included in the one thousand and fifty rupees). Thus, out of every rupee of his income the rich labourer will pay only **five paisa** in indirect taxes. The richer the man, the **smaller** is the share of his income that he pays in indirect taxes. That is why indirect taxation is **the most unfair** form of taxation. Indirect taxes are taxes on the poor. The farmers and workers together form nine-tenths of the population and pay nine-tenths or eight-tenths of the total indirect taxation. And, in all probability, the income of the labourers and workers amounts to no more than four-tenths of the whole national income! And so, the Social-Democrats demand the abolition of indirect taxation and the introduction of a **progressive** tax on incomes and inheritances. That means that the higher the income, the higher the tax. Those who have an income of a thousand rupees must pay one paisa in the rupee; if the income is two thousand, two paisa in the rupee must be paid, and so on. The smallest incomes (let us say incomes of under four hundred rupees) do not pay anything at all. The richest pay the highest taxes. Such a tax, **an income-tax,** or more exactly, a **progressive income-tax,** would be much fairer than indirect taxes. And that is why the Social-Democrats are striving to secure the abolition of indirect taxation and the introduction of a progressive income-tax. Of course, all the property-owners, all the Rich, object to this measure and resist it. Only through a firm alliance between the rural poor and the urban workers can this improvement be **won** from the Rich.

Finally, the **free education** of children, which the Social-Democrats demand, would be a very important improvement for the whole of the people and for the rural poor in particular. Today, there are far fewer schools in the country- side than in the towns and everywhere it is only the rich classes, only the Rich, who are in a position to give their children a good education. Only free and compulsory education for **all children** can get the people, at least to some extent, out of their present state of ignorance. The rural poor suffer most from this ignorance and stand in particular need of education. But, of course, we need real, free education and not the sort the officials and the priests want to give.

The Social-Democrats further demand that everybody shall have full and unrestricted right to profess any religion he pleases. Of the Asian countries, India and Pakistan are the only ones which have retained shameful laws against persons belonging to any other faith than the orthodox, laws against schematics, sectarians and Muslims. These laws either totally ban a certain religion or prohibit its propagation or deprives those who belong to it of certain rights. All these laws are as unjust, as arbitrary and as disgraceful as can be. Everybody must be perfectly free, not only to profess whatever religion he pleases, **but also to spread or change his religion**. No official should have the right even to ask anyone about his religion: that is a matter for each person's conscience and no one has any right to interfere. There should be no "established" religion or church. All religions and all churches should have equal status in law. The clergy of the various religions should be paid salaries by those who belong to their religions, but the state should not use state money to support any religion whatever, should not grant money to maintain any clergy, church, temples and mosques or any other. That is what the Social-Democrats are fighting for and until these measures are carried out without any reservation and without any subterfuge, the people will not be freed from the disgraceful police persecution of religion or from the no less disgraceful police hand-outs to any one of those religions.

We have seen what improvements the Social-Democrats are out to achieve for all the people and especially for the poor. Now let us see what improvements they strive to achieve for the workers; not only for factory and urban workers, but for agricultural workers too. The factory workers live in more cramped conditions; they work in large workshops, so it is easier for them to avail themselves of the assistance of educated Social-Democrats. For all these reasons, the urban workers started the struggle against the employers much earlier than the others and have achieved more considerable improvements; they have also obtained the passing of factory laws. But the Social-Democrats are fighting for the extension of these improvements to **all** the workers: to handicraftsmen both in town and country, who work for employers at home; to the wage-workers employed by petty masters and artisans; to workers in the building trades (carpenters, bricklayers, etc.); to lumbermen and unskilled labourers **and also the agricultural labourers**. All over Karnataka, all these workers are now beginning to unite, following the example of, and aided by, the factory workers, to unite for the struggle for better conditions of life, for a shorter working day, **for higher wages**. And the Social-Democratic Party has set itself the task of supporting **all** workers in their struggle for a better life, of helping them to organise (to unite) the most resolute and reliable workers in strong unions, of helping them by circulating pamphlets and leaflets, by sending experienced workers to those new to the movement and in general helping all the workers in every possible way. When we have won political liberty, we shall have our people in a national assembly of MLAs, worker deputies, Social-Democrats, and, like their comrades in other countries, they will demand laws for the benefit of the workers.

We shall not enumerate here **all** the improvements the Social-Democratic Party is striving to obtain for the workers: they have been set out in our programme and explained in detail in the pamphlet, **The Workers' Cause in Karnataka**. Here, it will be sufficient to mention the most important of those improvements. The, working day must not be longer than eight hours. One day a week must always be a day of rest. <u>Overtime must be absolutely banned, and so must night-work. Children up to the age of sixteen must he given free education, and, consequently, must not be allowed to work for hire until that age. Women must not work in trades injurious to their health. The employer must compensate the workers for all injury caused during work, for example, for injury caused when working on threshing-machines, winnowing-machines, and so forth. All wage-workers must always be paid **weekly** and not once in two months or once in a quarter as is often the case with agricultural labourers.</u> It is very important for the workers to be paid regularly every week and, moreover, to be paid in cash, and not in goods. Employers are very fond of making the workers accept all sorts of worthless goods at exorbitant prices in payment of wages; to put an end to this disgraceful practice, the payment of wages in goods must be absolutely prohibited by law. Further, aged workers must receive state pensions. By their labour the workers maintain all the rich classes, and the whole state, and that gives them as much right to pensions as government officials, who get pensions. To prevent employers from taking advantage of their position to disregard regulations introduced to protect the workers, inspectors must be appointed to supervise, not only the factories, but also the big landlord farms and, in general, all enterprises where wage-labour is employed. But those inspectors must not be government officials, or be appointed by ministers or governors or be in the service of the police. The inspectors must **be elected by the workers;** the state must pay salaries to persons who enjoy <u>the confidence of the workers and whom they have freely elected. These elected deputies of the workers must also see to it that the workers' dwellings are kept in proper condition, that the employers dare not compel the workers to live in what is like pigsties</u> or in mud huts (as is often the case with agricultural labourers), that the rules concerning the workers' rest are observed, and so on. It must not be forgotten, however, that no elected workers' deputies will be of any use as long as there is no political liberty, as long as the police are all-powerful, and are not responsible to the people. Everyone knows that at present the police will arrest without trial, not only workers' deputies but any worker who will dare speak in the name of all his fellow workers, expose breaches of the law or call on the workers to unite. But when we have political liberty, the workers' deputies will be of very great use.

All employers (factory owners, landlords, contractors, and rich labourers) should **be absolutely forbidden** to make any arbitrary deductions from the wages of their workers, for example, deductions for defective goods, deductions in the form of fines, etc. It is unlawful and tyrannical for employers **arbitrarily** to make deductions from workers' wages. The employer must not reduce a worker's wage by means of any deductions or in any way whatsoever. The employer should not be allowed to pass and execute judgement (a fine sort of judge, who pockets the deductions from the worker's wages!); he should appeal to a **proper court** and this court must consist of deputies elected by the workers and the employers in equal numbers. Only such a court will be able to judge fairly all the grievances of the employers against the workers and of the workers against the employers.

Such are the improvements the Social-Democrats are striving to obtain for the whole of the working class. The workers on every landed estate, on every farm, in the employ of every contractor, must meet and discuss with trustworthy persons what improvements they must strive to obtain and what demands they should advance (for the demands of the workers will, of course, be different at different factories, on different estates and with different con- tractors).

All over Karnataka **Social-Democratic committees** are helping the workers to formulate their demands in a clear and precise way and are helping them to issue printed leaflets where these demands are set out, so that they may be known to all workers and to the employers and the authorities. When the workers unite as one man in support of their demands, the employers always have to give way and agree to them. In the towns, the workers have already obtained many improvements in this way and now handicraftsmen, artisans and agricultural labourers are also beginning to unite (to organise) and fight for their demands. As long as we have no political liberty, we carry on the fight in secret, hiding from the police, who prohibit the publication of all leaflets and associations of workers. But when we have won political liberty, we shall carry on the fight on a wider scale and openly, so that working people all over Karnataka may unite and defend themselves more vigorously from oppression. The larger the number of workers who unite **in the workers' Social-Democratic Party,** the stronger will they be, the sooner will they be able to achieve the complete emancipation of the working class from all oppression, from all wage-labour, from all toil for the benefit of the Rich.

We have already said that the Social-Democratic Labour Party is striving to obtain improvements, not only for the workers, but also for **all the labourers.** Now, let us see what improvements it is striving to obtain for all the labourers.

13

What improvements are the Social-Democrats striving to obtain for all the Labourers?

To secure the complete emancipation of all working people, the rural poor must, in alliance with the urban workers, wage a fight against the whole of the Rich, including the rich labourers. The rich labourers will strive to pay their farm labourers as little as possible and make them work as long and as hard as possible; but the workers in town and villages will try to secure better wages, better conditions and regular rest periods for farm labourers working for the rich labourers. That means that the rural poor must form their own unions apart from the rich labourers. We have already said this and we shall always repeat it.

But in Karnataka, all labourers, rich and poor, are still bonded labourers in many respects; they are an **inferior, "black," tax-paying social-estate;** they are all bonded labourers of the police officers and tahsildar; very often they have to work for the landlord in payment for the use of the cut-off lands, watering places, pastures or meadows, just as they worked for the feudal lord under the slave-owning system. **All** the labourers want to be free of this new slavery; **all** of them want to have full rights; **all** of them hate the landlords, who still compel them to **perform slave labour,** to pay "labour rent" for the use of the gentry's land and pastures, watering places and meadows, to work also "for damage" done by straying cattle and to send their womenfolk to reap the landlord's field merely "for the honour of it." All this labour rent for the landlord is a heavier burden for the poor labourers than for the rich labourers. The rich labourer is sometimes able to pay the landlord money in lieu of this work, but as a rule even the rich labourer is badly squeezed by the landlord. Hence, the rural poor must fight side-by-side with the rich labourers against their lack of rights, against every kind of slave labour, against every kind of labour rent. We shall be able to abolish **all** bondage, **all** poverty only when we defeat the Rich **as a whole** (including the rich labourers). But there are forms of bondage which we can abolish **before that time**, because even the rich labourer suffers badly from them. There are many localities and many districts in Karnataka where very often all the labourers are still quite like bonded labourer. That is why all Karnataka workers and all <u>the rural poor</u> <u>must</u> **<u>fight with both hands and on two sides:</u>** <u>with one</u> **<u>hand—fight</u>** **<u>against all the rich</u>**<u>, in alliance with all the workers; and with the other</u> ***<u>hand—fight against the rural officials, against the feudal landlords,</u>*** in alliance with all the labourers. If the rural poor do not form their own union separately from the rich labourers they will be deceived by the rich labourers, who will become landlords themselves, while the landless poor will not only remain poor and without land but will not even be granted freedom to unite. If the rural poor do not fight side-by-side with the rich labourers against feudal bondage, they will remain fettered and tied down to one place, neither will they gain full freedom to unite with the urban workers.

The rural poor must first strike at the landlords and throw off at least the most vicious and most pernicious forms of feudal bondage; in this fight many of the rich labourers and adherents of the Rich will also take the side of the poor, because everybody is disgusted with the arrogance of the landlords. But as soon as we have curtailed the power of the landlords, the rich labourer will at once reveal his true character and stretch out greedy hands to grab everything; these are rapacious hands and they have already grabbed a great deal. Hence, we must be on our guard and form a strong, indestructible alliance with the urban workers. The urban workers will help to knock the old aristocratic habits out of the landlords and also tame the rich labourers a bit (as they have already somewhat tamed their own bosses, the factory owners). Without an alliance with the urban workers the rural poor will **never rid** themselves of all forms of bondage, want and poverty; except for the urban workers, there is **no one** to help the rural poor and they can count on no one but themselves. But there are improvements which we can obtain earlier, which we can obtain immediately, at the very outset of this great struggle. There are many forms of bondage in Karnataka which have long ceased to exist in other countries, and it is from this bondage imposed by the officials and landlords, this feudal bondage, that the **Karnatakala bourers as a whole** can free itself **immediately.**

Let us now see what improvements the workers' Social-Democratic Party is striving first of all to obtain so as to free the Karnatakala bourers as a whole from at least the most vicious forms of feudal bondage, and so as to untie the hands of the rural poor for their struggle against the Karnataka Rich as a whole.

The first demand of the workers' Social-Democratic Party is the immediate abolition of all land redemption payments, all quit-rent, and all the dues imposed upon the "tax-paying" labourers. When the committees of Capitalists (Adani and Ambani) and the Karnataka CM's government, consisting of Capitalists (Adani and Ambani), "emancipated" the labourers from slave dom, the labourers were compelled to **buy out their own** land, to buy out the land which they had tilled for generations! That was **robbery.** The committees of Capitalists (Adani and Ambani), assisted by the PRIME MINISTER and government, simply **robbed** the labourers. The PRIME MINISTER and government sent troops to many places to impose the title-deeds upon the labourers **by force,** to take military punitive measures against the labourers, who were unwilling to accept the curtailed "pauper" allotments. Without the help of the troops, without brutality and shootings, the committees of Capitalists (Adani and Ambani) would never have been able to rob the labourers in the brazen way they did at the time of the emancipation from slave dom and Covid 19. The labourers must always remember how they were cheated and robbed by those committees of land-owning Capitalists (Adani and Ambani), because even today the PRIME MINISTER and government always appoints committees of Capitalists (Adani and Ambani) or officials whenever it is a question of passing new laws concerning the labourers. The PRIME MINISTER recently issued a manifesto, in which he promises to revise and improve the laws concerning the labourers. Who will do the revising? Who will do the improving? Again the Capitalist, again the officials! The labourers will always be defrauded until they secure the setting up of **labourer committees** for the purpose of improving their conditions of life. It is time to put a stop to the landlords, tahsildar, and all kinds of officials lording it over the labourers! It is time to put a stop to this feudal dependence of the labourer upon every police officer, upon every drink-sodden scion of the Capitalist who is called a tahsildar, a police chief or a Governor! The labourers must demand freedom to manage their affairs **themselves,** freedom to consider, propose and carry out new laws **themselves.** The labourers must demand the setting-up of free, elected **labourer committees** and until they obtain this they will always be defrauded and robbed by the Capitalist and the officials. No one will free the labourers from the official leeches, if they do not free themselves, if they do not unite and take their fate into **their own** hands.

The Social-Democrats not only demand the complete and immediate abolition of land redemption payments, quit-rent, and imposts of all kinds; they also demand that money taken from the people in the form of land redemption payments should be **restituted to the people**. Hundreds of millions of rupees have been paid up by labourers all over Karnataka since the committees of Capitalists (Adani and Ambani). The labourers must demand that this money be returned to them. Let the government impose a special tax on the big landed Capitalist; let the land be taken from the temples, churches, the monasteries and from the Department of Revenue (i.e., from the PRIME MINISTER and Capitalists); let the State assembly of MLAs use this money for the benefit of the labourers. Nowhere in the world is the labourer so downtrodden or so impoverished as is in Karnataka. <u>Nowhere do millions of labourers die so horribly of starvation as they do in Karnataka. The labourers in Karnataka have been reduced to dying of starvation because they were robbed long ago by the committees of Capitalists (Adani and Ambani)</u>, and are being robbed to this day by being forced to pay tribute to the heirs of the feudal landlords every year in the form of redemption payments and quit-rent. The robbers must be made to answer for their crimes! Let money be taken away from the big landed Capitalist so as to provide effective relief for the famine-stricken. The starving labourer does not need charity, he does not need paltry doles; he must demand the return of the money he has paid for years and years to the landlords and to the state. The State assembly of MLAs and the labourer committees will then be able to give real and effective assistance to the starving.

When the working class has defeated the entire Rich, it will take the land away from the big proprietors and introduce **cooperative farming** on the big estates, so that the workers will farm the land together, in common, and freely elect delegates to manage the farms. They will have all kinds of labour-saving machines, and work in shifts for not more than eight (or even six) hours a day. The small labourer who prefers to carry on his farm in the old way on individual lines will not then produce for the market, to sell to the first comer, but for the workers' cooperatives; the small labourer will supply the workers' cooperatives with grain, meat, vegetables and the workers in return will provide him free of charge with machines, livestock, fertilisers, clothes and whatever else he needs. There will then be no struggle for money between the big and the small farmer; there will then be no working for hire for others; all workers will work for themselves, all improvements in methods of production and all machines will benefit the workers themselves and help to make their work easier and improve their standard of living.

But every sensible man understands that socialism cannot be attained at once: to attain it a fierce struggle must be waged against the entire Rich and all governments; all urban workers all over Karnataka must unite in a firm and unbreakable alliance with all the rural poor. That is a great cause and to thatcause it is worth devoting one's whole life. But until we have attained socialism, the big owner will always fight the small owner for money.

<u>The labourers have never received anything good from the officials, except beatings, extortions and bullying. The labourers will never receive anything good until they take their affairs into their own hands</u>, until they obtain complete equality of rights and complete liberty. If the labourers want their land to be communal, no one will dare to interfere with them; and they will voluntarily form an association which will include whomsoever they like, and on whatever terms they like; they will quite freely draw up a communal contract in whatever form they like. And let no official dare poke his nose into the communal affairs of the labourers. Let no one dare exercise his wits on the labourers and invent restrictions and prohibitions for them.

That is why the Social-Democratic workers warn the labourers:

Place no faith in any committees of Capitalists (Adani and Ambani) or in any commissions consisting of officials.

Demand a State Assembly of MLAs from Working class background.

Demand the establishment of labourer committees.

Free Education and Health Care to all the families whose incomeis less than 5 lakh rupees

When all have the right freely and fearlessly to express their opinions and their wishes in the State assembly of MLAs, in the labourer committees and in the newspapers, it will very soon be seen who is on the side of the working class and who is on the side of the Rich. Today, the great majority of the people do not think about these things at all; some conceal their real views, some do not yet know their own minds and some lie deliberately. But when this right has been won, everyone will begin to think about these things; there will be no reason for concealing anything and everything will soon become clear. We have already said that the Rich will draw the rich labourers to its side. The sooner and the more completely we succeed in abolishing slave bondage and the more real freedom the labourers obtain for themselves, the sooner will the rural poor unite among themselves and the sooner will the rich labourers unite with all the Rich. Let them unite: we are not afraid of that, although we know perfectly well that this will strengthen the rich labourers. But we, too, will unite and our union, the union between the rural poor and the urban workers, will embrace far more people. It will be a union of tens of millions against a union of hundreds of thousands. We also know that the Rich will try (it is already trying!) to attract the middle and even the small labourers to its side; it will try to deceive them, entice them, sow dissension among them and promise to raise each of them into the ranks of the rich. We have already seen the means and the deceit the Rich resort to in order to lure the middle labourer. We must, therefore, open the eyes of the rural poor beforehand, and consolidate in advance their separate union with the urban workers against the entire Rich.

Let every villager look around carefully. How often we hear the rich labourers talking against the Capitalist, against the landlords! How they complain of the oppression the people suffer from! Or of the landlords' land lying idle! How they love to talk (in private conversation) about what a good thing it would be if the labourers took possession of the land!

Can we believe what the rich labourers say? No. They do not want the land for the people; they want it for themselves. They have already got hold of a great deal of land, bought outright or rented and still they are not satisfied. **Hence, the rural poor will not long have to march side-by-side with the rich labourers against the landlords.** Only the first step will have to be taken in their company and after that their ways will part.

That is why we must draw a clear distinction between this first step and subsequent steps and our final and most important step.

The first step in the villages will be the complete emancipation of the labourer, full rights for the labourer and the establishment of labourer committees for the purpose of restoring the cut-off lands. But our final step will be the same in both town and country: **we shall take all the land and all the factories from the landlords and the Rich and set up a socialist society.** We shall have to go through a big struggle in the period between our first step and the final, **and whoever confuses the first step with the final weakens that struggle and unwittingly helps to hoodwink the rural poor.**

The rural poor will take the first step together with all the labourers: a few middlemen may fall out, perhaps one labourer in a hundred is willing to put up with any kind of bondage. But the overwhelming mass of the labourers will, as yet, advance as one whole: all the labourers want equal rights. Bondage to the landlords ties everyone hand and foot. But the final step will never be taken by all the labourers together: then, all the rich labourers will turn against the farm labourers. Then, it is a strong union of the rural poor and the **urban Social-Democratic workers** that we need. Whoever tells the labourers that they can take the first and the final step simultaneously is deceiving them. He forgets about the great struggle that is going on among the labourers themselves, the **great** struggle between the rural poor and the rich labourers.

That is why the Social-Democrats do not promise the labourers **immediately** a land flowing with milk and honey. That is why the Social-Democrats first of all demand complete freedom for the struggle, for the great, nation-wide struggle of the entire working class against the entire Rich. That is why the Social-Democrats advise a **small but sure first step.**

Some people think that our demand for the establishment of labourer committees for the purpose of restricting bondage and of restoring the cut-off lands is a sort of fence or barrier, as if we meant to say: stop, not a step farther! These people have given insufficient thought to what the Social-Democrats want. The demand for labourer committees to be set up for the purpose of restricting bondage and of restoring the cut off lands is not a barrier. It is a **door**. We must first pass through this door **in order to go farther,** to march along the wide and open road **to the very end,** to the complete emancipation of all working people in Karnataka. Until the labourers pass through this door they will remain in ignorance and bondage, without full rights, without complete and real liberty; they will not even be able to decide definitely among themselves who is the friend of the working man and who his enemy. That is why the Social-Democrats point to this door and say that the entire people must all together first force this door and smash it in. But there are people who call themselves Socialist-Revolutionaries, who also wish the labourer well, shout and make a noise, wave their arms about and want to help him, but they **do not see that door!** Those people are so blind that they even say: there is no need at all to give the labourer the right freely to dispose of his land! They wish the labourer well, but sometimes they argue exactly like the feudal die-hards! Such friends can be of little help. What is the use of wishing the labourer all the best if you don't clearly see the very first door that must be smashed? What is the use of wanting Socialism if you don't see how to enter on the road of a free, people's struggle for Socialism, not only in the towns, but also in the villages, not only **against the landlords, but also against the rich labourers in the village commune, the "Union"?**

That is why the Social-Democrats point so insistently to this first and nearest door. The difficult thing at this stage is not to express a lot of good wishes, but to point to the right road, to understand clearly **how the very first step should be taken.** All friends of the labourer have been talking and writing for the past forty years about the Karnatakala bourer being crushed by bondage and about his remaining a semi-slave. Long before there were any Social-Democrats in India, the friends of the labourer wrote many books describing how shamefully the landlords robbed and enslaved the farmers by means of the various cut-off lands. All honest people now realise that the labourer must be given assistance at once, immediately, that he must get at least some relief from this bondage; even officials in our police government are beginning to talk about this. The whole question is: **how to set about it, how to take the first step,** which door must be forced first?

To this question different people (among those who wish the labourer well) give two different answers. Every rural poor must try to understand these two answers as clearly as possible and form a definite and firm opinion about them. One answer is given by the Socialist-Revolutionaries. The first thing to be done, they say, is to develop all sorts of societies (cooperatives) among the labourers. The unity of the **Union** must be strengthened. Every labourer should not be given the right to dispose of his land freely. Let the rights of the commune, the **Union**, be extended, and let all the land in Karnataka gradually become communal land. The labourers must be granted every assistance to purchase land, so that the land may more easily pass from capital to labour.

 WHAT IS TO BE DONE ?

The Karnataka Government realises that some relief must be given to the labourers, but it wants to make shift with trifles; it wants everything to be done by the officials. The labourers must be on the alert, because commissions of officials will cheat them just as they were cheated by the committees of Capitalists (Adani and Ambani). The labourers must demand the election of free labourer committees. The important thing is not to expect improvement from the officials, but for the labourers to take their fate into their own hands. Let us at first take only one step, at first abolish only the vicious forms of bondage—so that the labourers should become conscious of their strength, so that they should freely reach a common agreement and unite! No honest person can deny that the cut-off lands often serve as the instruments of the most outrageous slave bondage. No honest person can deny that our demand is the primary and fairest of demands: let the labourers freely elect **their own** committees, without the officials, for the purpose of abolishing all slave bondage.

In the free labourer committees (just as in the free all-Karnataka assembly of MLAs) the Social-Democrats will at once do all in their power to consolidate a distinct union of the rural poor with the urban poor. The Social-Democrats will make a stand for all measures for the benefit of the rural poor and will help them to follow up the first step, as quickly as possible and as unitedly as possible, with the second and the third step, and so on to the very end, to the complete **victory of the poor**. But can we say today, at once, what demand will be appropriate tomorrow for the second step? No, we cannot, because we do not know what stand will be taken tomorrow by the rich labourers and by many educated people who are concerned with all kinds of cooperatives and with the land passing from capital to labour.

Perhaps they will not yet succeed in reaching an understanding with the landlords on the morrow; perhaps they will want to put an end to landlord rule completely. Very good! The Social-Democrats would very much like this to happen, and they will advise rural and urban poor to demand that all the land be taken from the landlords and transferred to the free people's state. The Social-Democrats will vigilantly see to it that the rural poor are not cheated in the course of this, and that they still further consolidate their forces for the final struggle for the complete emancipation of the poor.

But things may turn out quite differently. In fact, it is more likely that they will turn out differently. On the very day after the worst forms of bondage have been restricted and curtailed, the rich labourers and many educated people may unite with the landlords, and then the entire rural rich will rise against the entire rural poor. In that event it would be ridiculous for us to fight only the landlords. We would then have to fight the entire rich and demand first of all the greatest possible freedom and elbow-room for this fight, demand better conditions of life for the workers in order to facilitate this struggle.

In any case, whichever way things turn out, our first, our principal and indispensable task is **to strengthen the alliance of the rural poor and semi-poor with the urban poor.** For this alliance we need at once, immediately, **complete political liberty for the people, complete equality of rights for the labourers and the abolition of slave bondage.** And when that alliance is established and strengthened, we shall easily expose all the deceit the rich resorts to in order to attract the middle labourer; we shall easily and quickly take the second, the third and the last step against the entire rich, against all the government forces, and we shall unswervingly march to victory and rapidly achieve the **complete emancipation of all working people.**

14

The Class Struggle
in the Villages

What is the **class struggle?** It is a struggle of one part of the people against the other; a struggle waged by the masses of those who have no rights, are oppressed and engage in toil, against the privileged, the oppressors and drones; a struggle of the wage-labourers, or poor, against the property-owners or rich. This great struggle has always gone on and is now going on in the Karnataka villages too, although not everyone sees it and although not everyone understands its significance. In the period of slave dom, the entire mass of the labourers fought against their oppressors, the landlord class, which was protected, defended and supported by the PRIME MINISTER and government. The labourers were then unable to unite and were utterly crushed by ignorance; they had no helpers and brothers among the urban workers; nevertheless, they fought as best they could. They were not deterred by the brutal persecution of the government, were not daunted by punitive measures and bullets and did not believe the priests, who tried with all their might to prove that slave dom was approved by Holy Scriptures and sanctioned by God, the labourers rose in rebellion, now in one place and now in another, and at last the government yielded, fearing a general uprising of all the labourers.

Slave dom was abolished, but not altogether. The labourers remained without rights, remained an inferior, tax-paying, "black" social-estate, remained in the clutches of slave bondage. Unrest among the labourers continues; they continue to seek complete, real freedom. Meanwhile, after the abolition of slave dom, a new class struggle arose, the ***struggle of the poor against the rich.*** Wealth increased, railways and big factories were built, the towns grew still more populous and more luxurious, but all this wealth was appropriated by a very few, while the people became poorer all the time, became ruined, starved, and had to leave their homes to go and hire themselves out for wages. The urban workers started a great, new struggle of all the poor against all the rich. The urban workers have united in the **Social-Democratic Party** and are waging their struggle stubbornly, staunchly, and solidly, advancing step-by- step, preparing for the great final struggle and demanding political liberty for all the people.

At last the labourers, too, lost patience. In the spring of last year, the labourers of Mandya, Shivamogga, and other districts rose against the landlords, broke open their barns, shared the contents among themselves, distributed among the starving the grain that had been sown and reaped by the labourers but appropriated by the landlords and demanded a new division of the land. The labourers could no longer bear the endless oppression and began to seek a better lot. The labourers decided—and quite rightly so—that it was better to die fighting the oppressors than to die of starvation without a struggle. But they did not win a better lot for themselves. The PRIME MINISTER and government proclaimed them common rioters and robbers (for having taken from the robber landlords grain which the labourers themselves had sown and reaped!); the PRIME MINISTER and government sent troops against them as against an enemy, and the labourers were defeated; labourers were shot down, many were killed; peasants were brutally flogged, many were flogged to death; they were tortured worse than the Israelites tortured their enemies, the Gaza people. The PRIME MINISTER's envoys, the governors, were the worst torturers, real executioners.

The labourers fought in a just cause. The Karnataka working class will always honour the memory of the martyrs who were shot down and flogged to death by the PRIME MINISTER's servants. Those martyrs fought for the freedom and happiness of the working people. The labourers were defeated, but they will rise again and again, and will not lose heart because of this first defeat. The class-conscious workers will do all in their power to inform the largest possible number of working people in town and country about the labourers' struggle and to help them prepare for another and more successful struggle. The class-conscious workers will

 What Is To Be Done ?

do all in their power to help the labourers **clearly to understand why the first labourer uprising was crushed and what must be done in order to secure victory for the labourers and workers and not for the PRIME MINISTER's servants.**

<u>The labourer uprising was crushed because it was an uprising of an ignorant and politically unconscious mass, an uprising without clear and definite **political** demands, i.e., without the demand for a change in the **political** order. The labourer uprising was crushed because *no preparations had been made for it.*</u> The labourer uprising was crushed because the rural poor had not yet allied themselves with the urban poor. Such were the three causes of the labourers' first failure. To be successful an insurrection must have a conscious political aim; preparations must be made for it in advance; it must spread throughout the whole of Karnataka and be in alliance with the urban workers. And every step in the struggle of the urban workers, every Social-Democratic pamphlet or newspaper, every speech made by a class-conscious worker to the rural poor will bring nearer the time when the insurrection will be repeated and end in victory.

The labourers rose without a conscious political aim, simply because they could not bear their sufferings any longer, because they did not want to die like dumb brutes, without resistance. The labourers had suffered so much from every manner of robbery, oppression and torment that they could not but believe, if only for a moment, the vague rumours about the PRIME MINISTER's mercy; they could not but believe that every sensible man would regard it as just that grain should be distributed among starving people, among those who had worked all their lives for others, had sown and reaped and were now dying of starvation, while the "gentry's" barns were full to bursting. The labourers seemed to have forgotten that the best land and all the factories had been seized by the rich, by the landlords and the rich, precisely for the purpose of compelling the starving people to work for them. The labourers forgot that not only do the priests preach sermons in defence of the rich class, but the entire PRIME MINISTER and government, with its host of bureaucrats and soldiers, rises in its defence. The PRIME MINISTER and government re- minded the labourers of that. With brutal cruelty, the PRIME MINISTER and government showed the labourers what state power is, whose servant and whose protector it is. We need only remind the labourers of this lesson more often, and they will easily understand why it is necessary *to change the political order* and why we need **political liberty.** Labourer uprisings will have a conscious political aim when that is understood by larger and larger numbers of people, when every labourer who can read and write and who thinks for himself becomes familiar with the **three principal demands** which must be fought for first of all. The first demand—the convocation of a **State Assembly of MLAs for the purpose of establishing popular elective government in Karnataka in place of the autocratic government.** The second demand—**free education and free health-care**. The third demand—**recognition by law of the labourers' complete equality of rights with the other social-estates and the institution of elected labourer committees** with the primary object of abolishing all forms of slave bondage. Such are the chief and fundamental demands of the Social-Democrats, and it will now be very easy for the labourers to understand them, to understand **what to begin with** in the struggle for the people's freedom. When the labourers understand these demands, they will also understand that long, persistent and persevering **preparations** must be made in advance for the struggle, not in isolation, but together with the workers in the towns— the Social-Democrats.

Let every class-conscious worker and labourer rally around himself the most intelligent, reliable and fearless comrades. Let him strive to explain to them what the Social-Democrats want, so that every one of them may understand the struggle that must be waged and the demands that must be advanced. Let the class-conscious Social-Democrats begin gradually, cautiously, but unswervingly, to teach the labourers the doctrine of Social-Democracy, give them Social-Democratic pamphlets to read and explain those pamphlets at small gatherings of trustworthy people.

But the doctrine of Social-Democracy must not be taught from books alone; every instance, every case of oppression and injustice we see around us must be used for this purpose. The Social-Democratic doctrine is one of struggle against all oppression, all robbery, all injustice. Only he who knows the causes of oppression and **who all his life fights every case of oppression** is a real Social-Democrat. How can this be done? When they gather in their town or village, class-conscious Social-Democrats must themselves decide how it must be done to the best advantage of the entire working class. To show how it must be done, I shall cite one or two examples. Let us suppose that a Social-Democratic worker has come on a visit to his village or that some urban Social-Democratic worker has come to any village. The entire village is in the clutches of the neighbouring landlord, like a fly in a spider's web; it has always been in this state of bondage and cannot escape from it. The worker must at once pick out the most sensible, intelligent and trustworthy labourers, those who are seeking justice and will not be frightened by the first police agent who comes along and explain to them the causes of this hopeless bondage, tell them how the landlords cheated the labourers and robbed them with the aid of the committees of Capitalists (Adani and Ambani) , tell them how strong the rich are and how they are supported by the PRIME MINISTER and government, and also tell them about the demands of the Social-Democratic workers. When the labourers understand all these simple things they must all put their heads together and discuss whether it is possible to put up united resistance to the landlord, whether it is possible to put forward the first and principal demands (in the same way as the urban workers present their demands to the factory owners). If the landlord holds one big village, or several villages, in bondage, the best thing would be to obtain, through trustworthy people, a **leaflet** from the nearest Social-Democratic committee. In the leaflet, the Social-Democratic committee will correctly describe, from the very beginning, the bondage the labourers suffer from and formulate their most immediate demands (reduction of rent paid for land, proper rates and not half-rates, of pay for winter hire or less persecution for damage done by straying cattle or various other demands). From such a leaflet all labourers who can read and write will get to know very well what the issue is and those who cannot read will have it explained to them. The labourers will then clearly see that the Social-Democrats support them, that the Social-Democrats condemn all robbery. The labourers will then begin to understand what relief, if only slight, but relief for all that, can be obtained now, at once, if all stand together and what big improvements for the whole country they must seek to obtain by a great struggle in conjunction with the Social-Democratic workers in the towns. The labourers will then prepare more and more for that great struggle; they will learn how to find trustworthy people and how to stand unitedly for their demands. Perhaps they may sometimes succeed in organising a strike, as the urban workers do. True, this is more difficult in the villages than in the towns, but it is sometimes possible for all that; in other countries there have been successful strikes; for instance, in the busy seasons, when the landlords and rich farmers are badly in need of hands. If the rural poor are prepared to strike, if an agreement has long been reached about the general demands, if those demands have been explained in leaflets or properly explained at meetings, all will stand together, and the landlord will have to yield or at least put some curb on his greed. If the strike is unanimous and is called during the busy season, the landlord and even the authorities with their troops, will find it hard to do anything—time will be lost, the landlord will be threatened with ruin and he will soon become more tractable. Of course, strikes are a new thing and new things do not come off well at first. The urban workers, too, did not know how to fight unitedly at first; they did not know what demands to put forward in common; they simply went out to smash machinery and wreck a factory. But now the workers have learned to conduct a united struggle. Every new job must first be learned. The workers now understand that immediate relief can be obtained only if they stand together; meanwhile, the people are getting used to offering united resistance and are preparing more and more for the great and decisive struggle. Similarly, the labourers will learn to stand up to the worst robbers, to be united in their demands for some measure of relief and to prepare gradually, persistently and everywhere for the great battle for freedom. The number of class-conscious workers and labourers will constantly grow and the unions of rural Social-Democrats will become stronger and stronger; every case of bondage to the landlord, of extortion by the priest, of police brutality and bureaucratic oppression, will increasingly serve to open the eyes of the people, accustom them to putting up united resistance and to the idea that it is necessary to change the political order by force.

At the very beginning of this pamphlet we said that at the present time the urban workers come out into the streets and squares and publicly demand **freedom**, that they inscribe on their banners and cry out: "Down with the autocracy!" The day will soon come when the urban workers will rise not merely to march shouting through the streets, but for the great and final struggle; when the workers will declare as one man: "We shall win freedom, or die in the fight!"; when the places of the hundreds who have been killed, fallen in the fight will be taken by thousands of fresh and still more resolute fighters. And the labourers, too, will then rise all over Karnataka and go to the aid of the urban workers, will fight to the end for the freedom of the workers and labourers. The PRIME MINISTER's hordes will be unable to withstand that onslaught. Victory will go to the working people and the working class will march along the wide, spacious road to the liberation of all working people from any kind of oppression. The working class will use its freedom to fight for socialism!

*****

 WHAT IS TO BE DONE ?